Y0-AFA-698

A TREASURY OF
GAMES

Contents

A TREASURY OF GAMES

by CARL WITHERS

(Originally published under the title *Ready or Not, Here I Come*)

Illustrated by GARRY MACKENZIE

GROSSET & DUNLAP • **Publishers** • **NEW YORK**

1971 PRINTING

(Originally published under the title *Ready or Not, Here I Come*)

Library of Congress Catalog Card Number: 78-86694

ISBN: 0-448-02978-2 (TRADE EDITION) ISBN: 0-448-03113-2 (LIBRARY EDITION)

Copyright 1947 by Thomas Y. Crowell Co. © 1964 by Carl Withers
All rights reserved under International and Pan-American Copyright Conventions.
Published simultaneously in Canada.   Printed in the United States of America.

WHO'LL BE IT?

Counting Out

Many games require an It as leader, or to perform the hardest task in the game. The most frequent way of choosing It is with a counting-out rhyme. In fact, counting out is a very amusing game in its own right.

The players gather about someone who recites a rhyme, pointing to himself and all the rest in turn as he chants each word. By one method of counting out, the player on whom the last word falls is It. By another method, he is out, and the rhyme is repeated until only one player is left to be It. Here are some rhymes for counting out:

> Eenie, meenie, minie, mo,
> Catch a rabbit by the toe.
> If he hollers, let him go,
> Eenie, meenie, minie, mo.

Apples, peaches, pears, and plums;
Tell me when your birthday comes.
J-A-N-U-A-R-Y (or whatever other month is given
    as birth month by the one on whom "comes" falls).

Ibbity, bibbity, sibbity, Sam,
Ibbity, bibbity, steamboat.
Up the river, down the river,
Out goes *you*.

Intery, mintery, cutery, corn,
Apple seed and apple thorn,
Wire, briar, limber lock,
How many geese to make a flock?
One flew east and one flew west;
One flew over the cuckoo's nest.

One-ery, two-ery, zickery, zan,
Hollow bone, crack a bone, nine-ery, ten;
Spinkum, spankum, winkum, wankum,
Twiddle-um, twaddle-um, twenty-one.

One, two, three, four, five, six, seven;
All good children go to heaven.

One, two, three, four, five, six, seven, eight;
All bad children have to wait.

Icka, bicka, balinda,
The monkey washed the winda.
The winda broke,
The monkey got soaked,
Icka, bicka, balinda.

Eenie, meenie, minie, mo,
Catch a tiger by the toe.
If he hollers, make him pay
Fifty dollars every day.
My mother says to pick this one;
O-U-T spells out goes you,
Right in the middle of the red, white and blue.

One, two, three,
Mother caught a flea.
Flea died and mother cried.
One, two, three.

E-ry, i-ry, ickery, Ann,
Bobtail, vinegar, tickle and tan,
Hare-um, scare-um, buckram, bare-um,
Tea, tie, toe, tis.

Two, four, six, eight,
Mary at the garden gate,
Eating cherries off a plate;
Two, four, six, eight.

Dickery, dickery, dare,
The pig flew up in the air;
The man in brown
Soon brought him down;
Dickery, dickery, dare.

William A. Trimbletoe,
He's a good fisherman.
Catches fish,
Puts 'em in a dish.
Catches hens,
Puts 'em in pens.
Some lay eggs
And some lay none.
Wire, briar, limberlock,
Three geese in a flock;
One flew East,
And one flew West,
And one flew over the cuckoo's nest.
O-U-T spells out;
Go out, you dirty dishrag, you.

Little boy, driving cattle,
Don't you hear his money rattle?
One, two, three,
Out goes he (or she).

Eenie, meenie, minie, mo,
Catch a monkey by the toe;
If he hollers, make him pay
Fifty dollars every day.
My mother told me to choose the very best one.
Take a peach, take a plum,
Take a stick of chewing gum.

My mother and your mother live across the way —
One-fifteen North Broadway.
Every night they have a fight
And this is what they say:

   Acka, backa, soda cracka,
   Acka, backa, boo.
   If your daddy chews tobacco,
   Out goes Y-O-U.

Monkey in the matchbox,
Don't you hear him holler?
Take him to the station house,
And make him pay a dollar.

One, two, three, four, five,
I caught a fish alive.
Six, seven, eight, nine, ten,
I let it go again.

As I went up the apple tree,
All the apples fell on me.
Bake a pudding, bake a pie,
Did you ever tell a lie?
Yes, you did, you know you did;
You broke your mother's teapot lid.
L-I-D — that spells lid.

Eenie, meenie, tipsy, teeny,
Alma, Jacky, Josephiny.
My mother told me to choose this one,
Because she is the very best *one*.

Engine, engine, number nine,
Running on Chicago line;
If the train should jump the track,
Do you want your money back?

Monkey, monkey, bottle of beer,
How many monkeys have we here?
One, two, three,
Out goes he (or she).

Counting Out Feet

Sometimes all the players stand in a half-circle, except one who bends over and counts out their feet. Whatever foot the last word of the rhyme falls on is moved back, out of the counting. The rhyme is repeated until only one foot is left, and its owner is It.

> Johnson, Johnson,
> Come to the table.
> You are out!
>
> Fifty horses in a stable —
> And you are out.

Rumble, Rumble

The players gather in a close circle and extend their index fingers to form a "pot." Stirring one of his fingers in the pot, a player says, "Rumble, rumble in the pot." Then he counts each finger in turn, including his own, and recites:

> Rumble, rumble in the pot,
> Take one out and leave it hot.

The finger on which the word "hot" falls is out. The player repeats the rhyme until only one finger is left — belonging to It.

One Potato

One potato, two potatoes,
Three potatoes, four;
Five potatoes, six potatoes,
Seven potatoes, *more.*

Players put forward their fists, and one player counts off the fists, his own included, with this rhyme. Each time he reaches the word "more," a fist is withdrawn and put behind its owner's back. Finally, only one fist is left. The owner must be It.

Alphabet It

This is an entertaining variation on counting out. The players line up and one of them recites the alphabet, pointing to each player in turn as he says a letter. If a player's last name begins with the letter that falls on him, he is out. The alphabet is repeated until only one player is left. He is It.

Number It

A player cries, "Number!" and another player shouts a number. It should be not very large, but greater than the number of players. Then the leader counts round the circle, "One, two, three," etc. The player on whom the chosen number falls is It.

Stone Out

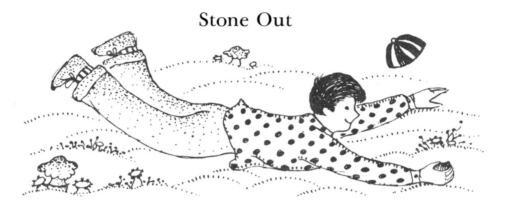

A player picks up a small stone and says, "Stone, stone, I'm out!" and tosses the stone away. The rest scramble to get the stone. Whoever gets it repeats the same words and throws the stone down, and there is another scramble. The game continues until the last player to get the stone becomes It.

Holders

A player hides a small stone in his hand and cries "Holders!" The other players shout "First!" "Second!" etc. The player holding the stone asks the "First" player to tap the hand he thinks the stone is in. If he guesses right, the "Holder" is out and "First" becomes the holder. He then hides the stone and turns to "Second." If "First" guesses wrong, however, *he* is out, and the original holder turns to "Second." The player who holds the stone last is It.

Longest or Shortest

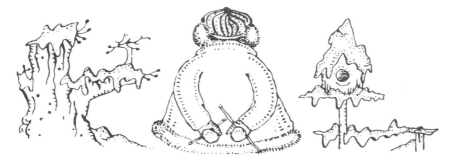

A player holds two straws or sticks behind him and asks another player to choose the hand with the longest or the shortest. The winner is out and the loser asks another player to choose. The last loser is It.

Short Sticks

Make a small heap of broken sticks. All the players reach into the heap at once for a stick. The one who draws the shortest (or the longest) stick is It.

Smallest Leaf

All the players close their eyes and each plucks a leaf from a bush. The player with the smallest leaf is It.

One, Two, Three, Shoot!

When a player cries, "One, two, three, shoot!" all thrust out from one to ten fingers each. Someone counts the extended fingers and then counts round the circle until he reaches that number. The player on whom the number falls is It.

Heads or Tails

This is much like *Holders,* but simpler. A player asks another player to guess "Heads" or "Tails" and throws out a coin. The winner goes out and the loser continues with the next player. The last loser is It.

Getting Out of It

An old taunt goes:

> You're It, you're It,
> You've got a fit,
> And don't know how
> To get out of It.

But sometimes the player chosen to be It can shout "Not It!" and get another chance. Then all the players go behind It, who must not look around. One player creeps up close to It's back, makes a circle of his left thumb and index finger, and pushes his right index finger through the circle into the small of It's back. In a disguised voice he says, "I made a little hole and put my finger in it," and then retreats to the group.

Now It turns around. All the players hold out their right index fingers and say, "This finger did it!" If It guesses whose finger actually did it, he is out, and a new It has to be chosen.

SINGING GAMES

I-Tisket I-Tasket

The players join hands in a circle. The one who is It runs round the circle, carrying a handkerchief and singing:

> I-tisket I-tasket,
> A green and yellow basket,
> I wrote a letter to my love,
> And on the way I dropped it.
> I dropped it, I dropped it,
> And on the way I dropped it.
> Somebody here has picked it up
> And put it in your pocket;
> It isn't you, it isn't you —
> *It's you!* (Spoken.)

On the words "It's you!" It drops the handkerchief behind a player and continues running. That player picks up the handkerchief and runs round the circle in the other direction. Both try to reach the vacant place in the circle. The one who gets there first joins the circle, and the loser is It for the next game.

The same game, played without the song, is called *Drop the Handkerchief*.

Oats, Peas, Beans, and Barley Grows

1. Oats, peas, beans, and barley grows,
   Oats, peas, beans, and barley grows,
   You nor I nor nobody knows
   How oats, peas, beans, and barley grows.

2. Here the farmer sows his seed,
   Then he stands and takes his ease,
   Stamps his foot and claps his hand,
   And turns around to view his land.

3. Waiting for a partner,
   Waiting for a partner,
   Choose one in out of the ring,
   While the others dance and sing.

4. Now you're married you must obey,
   You must be true to all you say,
   You must be kind, you must be good,
   And make your husband chop the wood.

The players choose a Farmer, then form a circle and move around him, singing stanza 1. In stanza 2, the Farmer performs all the actions named, and the players in the circle stop and imitate him. The circle moves again while singing stanza 3, and the Farmer chooses a partner. In stanza 4, the Farmer and his Wife bow and kneel, and then rise.

A new Farmer is chosen to repeat the game.

Where Has My Little Dog Gone?

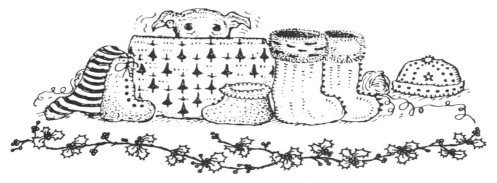

The players join hands and circle round the Master, who sings:

> Oh, where, oh, where has my little dog gone?
> Oh, where, oh, where can he be?
> With his ears cut short and his tail cut long —
> Oh, where, oh, where is he?

While singing, the Master pretends to be looking everywhere for his dog. On the final "he," everybody stops. The player whom the Master faces is the Dog. He drops the hands of his neighbors. The circle closes up again, and the Dog starts running in and out of the circle, or around it. The Master chases him, and must follow the Dog's path exactly. When he is finally caught, the Dog becomes Master for the next game, and the latter joins the circle.

Needle's Eye

Needle's eye,
That doth supply
The thread that runs so true;
Many a beau
Have I let go,
Because I wanted *you*.

All but two players form a circle. These two go aside to select secret names — for example, "orange" and "banana." Then one goes inside the circle, the other stands outside, and they clasp hands across a pair of joined arms. Now they start singing, lifting their arms up high for the circle to march through.

When they reach the word "you," they catch someone between their arms. They take that player aside and ask him, "Do you like oranges or bananas better?" When he chooses, he is told which one of the two players to stand behind.

The game goes on like this until everybody is caught and is standing behind one or the other of the two players. Then there is a tug of war between the two lines.

Looby Loo

To play this charming old game, the players clasp hands and form a ring. Then everyone sings the song, following the instructions for each line.

1. Here we dance looby, looby,   (*Alternate weight on feet, throwing free foot over other.*)

Here we dance looby light,
Here we dance looby loo,   (*Dance to left, halfway round circle.*)

All on a Saturday night.   (*Dance to right, halfway round circle.*)

I put my right hand in,   (*Thrust right hand into circle.*)
I put my right hand out,   (*Pull right hand out.*)
I give my right hand a shake, shake, shake,   (*Shake the right hand away from circle.*)
And turn myself about.   (*Turn round and take hold of your neighbors' hands.*)

2. Here we dance looby, looby,
   Here we dance looby light,
   Here we dance looby loo,
   All on a Saturday night.
   I put my left hand in,
   I put my left hand out,
   I give my left hand a shake,
               shake, shake,
   And turn myself about.

(For first four lines, follow directions for the first four lines above.)

(Follow directions for second four lines above, but use your left hand instead of your right.)

3. ... I put my two hands in ...
4. ... I put my right foot in ...
5. ... I put my left foot in ...
6. ... I put my right ear in ...
7. ... I put my left ear in ...
8. ... I put my little head in ...
9. ... I put my whole self in ...

(Suit actions to words in all the following stanzas.)

Mulberry Bush

Here we go round the mulberry bush,
The mulberry bush, the mulberry bush,
Here we go round the mulberry bush,
So early in the morning.

This is the way we wash our clothes,
Wash our clothes, wash our clothes,
This is the way we wash our clothes,
So early Monday morning.

This is the way we iron our clothes,
Iron our clothes, iron our clothes,
This is the way we iron our clothes,
So early Tuesday morning.

This is the way we scrub our floor,
Scrub our floor, scrub our floor,
This is the way we scrub our floor,
So early Wednesday morning.

This is the way we mend our clothes,
Mend our clothes, mend our clothes,
This the way we mend our clothes,
So early Thursday morning.

This is the way we sweep our house,
Sweep our house, sweep our house,
This is the way we sweep our house,
So early Friday morning.

This is the way we bake our bread,
Bake our bread, bake our bread,
This is the way we bake our bread,
So early Saturday morning.

This is the way we go to church,
Go to church, go to church,
This is the way we go to church,
So early Sunday morning.

The players clasp hands and circle around, singing the first stanza. In all the following stanzas, each player imitates the action as he sings. But at the end of each "So early——morning," he spins around in his place in the circle.

Nuts in May

The tune is the same as for *Mulberry Bush,* but the words and the game are very different.

1. Here we come gathering nuts in May,
   Nuts in May, nuts in May;
   Here we come gathering nuts in May,
   On a cold and frosty morning.

2. Whom will you have for nuts in May,
   Nuts in May, nuts in May?
   Whom will you have for nuts in May,
   On a cold and frosty morning?

3. We'll have *Mary* for nuts in May,
    Nuts in May, nuts in May;
    We'll have *Mary* for nuts in May,
    On a cold and frosty morning.

4. Whom will you send to take her away,
    Take her away, take her away?
    · Whom will you send to take her away,
    On a cold and frosty morning?

5. We'll send *Robert* to take her away,
    Take her away, take her away;
    We'll send *Robert* to take her away,
    On a cold and frosty morning.

The players form two lines, facing each other. One line sings the first stanza, moving toward the opposite line and back again. Then the second line sings the next stanza, moving forward and backward in the same way. The first line sings stanza 3, naming someone from the other line. The second line sings stanza 4. The first responds with 5.

The two players chosen go to the center, between the two lines, and have a tug of war. The loser is led back as a captured "nut" to the winner's line.

Now the whole song is repeated, but the *second* line starts it this time.

The game continues until every player has been chosen for a tug of war. The winning side is the line that captured the most "nuts" from the other.

Frog Pond

Come when the moon is up!
It's pleasant out here on the bank.
Come stick your heads out of the tank,
And let us, before we sup,
   Go kwok, kwok, kwok.
And let us, before we sup,
   Go kwok, kwok, kwok.

Hush! There comes the waddling duck!
He's coming, we'd better not stay.
We'd better be hopping away;
If we don't, he'll gobble us up,
   With a kwok, kwok, kwok.
If we don't, he'll gobble us up,
   With a kwok, kwok, kwok.

34

A player is chosen to be the Duck. The rest are Frogs. Each Frog then selects a "den," or safety spot, at a little distance from a central "frog pond." Now the Duck goes away, and the players hop around the frog pond — singing the first stanza.

As they start the second stanza, the Duck waddles toward them, and the Frogs try to hop safely to their dens before the Duck can catch them. The Frog that gets caught becomes the Duck for the next game.

Farmer in the Dell

The farmer in the dell,
The farmer in the dell,
Hey-o, the derry-o,
The farmer in the dell.

The farmer takes a wife,
The farmer takes a wife,
Hey-o, the derry-o,
The farmer takes a wife.

The wife takes a child,
The wife takes a child,
Hey-o, the derry-o,
The wife takes a child.

The child takes a nurse,
The child takes a nurse,
Hey-o, the derry-o,
The child takes a nurse.

The nurse takes a dog,
The nurse takes a dog,
Hey-o, the derry-o,
The nurse takes a dog.

The dog takes a cat,
The dog takes a cat,
Hey-o, the derry-o,
The dog takes a cat.

The cat takes a rat,
The cat takes a rat,
Hey-o, the derry-o,
The cat takes a rat.

The rat takes a cheese,
The rat takes a cheese,
Hey-o, the derry-o,
The rat takes a cheese.

The cheese stands alone,
The cheese stands alone,
Hey-o, the derry-o,
The cheese stands alone.

A Farmer is chosen, and the rest of the players circle around him, singing the song as they go. In the second stanza the Farmer chooses a Wife, and the Wife moves into the center of the circle with him. In the same way, the Wife chooses a Child, the Child chooses a Nurse, and so on, until finally the Cheese enters the circle. The circle, of course, gets smaller and smaller. With the last stanza, "The cheese stands alone," everybody jumps up and down and claps hands loudly at the poor Cheese. But he gets to be Farmer in the next game.

London Bridge

Two players form the arch of the bridge by joining their hands and raising them high. The rest form a circle and march under the bridge. All sing. On the word "lady" in each stanza, the two at the bridge drop their arms and catch someone. They whisper to him, "Will you take silver or gold?" They have already decided which word belongs to each of them, and when the captive chooses he is told whom to stand behind.

When all the players are caught, they line up behind their leaders and have a tug of war.

1. London Bridge is falling down, falling down, falling down,
   London Bridge is falling down, my fair lady.

2. Build it up with iron bars, iron bars, iron bars,
   Build it up with iron bars, my fair lady.

3. Iron bars will rust away . . .

4. Build it up with needles and pins . . .

5. Pins and needles rust away . . .

6. Build it up with penny loaves . . .

7. Penny loaves will tumble down . . .

8. Build it up with gold and silver . . .

9. Gold and silver I've not got . . .

10. Here's a prisoner we have got . . .

11. What's the prisoner done to you . . .

12. Stole my watch and broke my crown . . .

13. What'll you take to set him free . .

14. A hundred pounds will set him free . . .

15. A hundred pounds we have not got . . .

16. Then off to prison he must go . . .

39

Muffin Man

Oh, do you know the muffin man,
The muffin man, the muffin man,
Oh, do you know the muffin man,
Who lives in Drury Lane?

Oh, yes, I know the muffin man,
The muffin man, the muffin man,
Oh, yes, I know the muffin man,
Who lives in Drury Lane.

Now two [four, eight . . . all] of us know the muffin man,
The muffin man, the muffin man,
Now two [four, eight . . . all] of us know the muffin man,
Who lives in Drury Lane.

Make a circle and skip to the left round a player in the center — as you sing the first stanza. The center player answers with the second stanza, skipping to the right inside the circle. At the end, he chooses a partner. These two join hands and sing the third stanza ("Now two of us know . . ."), skipping to the right. The circle, meanwhile, keeps on moving to the left. At the end of the third stanza, both center players choose new partners. These four players form a ring inside the larger one and skip to the right, singing "Now four of us know. . . ."

This goes on until all the players have been taken into the inner ring. Then everybody sings "Now all of us know. . . ."

While all this is happening, the original circle closes in as long as possible around the inner ring. But when its members can no longer reach each other's hands, they separate and keep on skipping round the inner ring until all have been chosen to join it.

Lazy Mary

1. Lazy Mary, will you get up?
   Will you, will you, will you get up?
   Lazy Mary, will you get up?
   Will you get up today?

2. No, Mother, I won't get up,
   I won't, I won't, I won't get up,
   No, Mother, I won't get up,
   I won't get up today.

3. What will you give me for my breakfast,
   If I get up, if I get up?
   What will you give me for my breakfast,
   If I get up today?

4. A slice of bread and a cup of tea,
   A slice of bread and a cup of tea,
   A slice of bread and a cup of tea,
   If you'll get up today.

5. What will you give me for my dinner?
   What will you give me for my dinner?
   What will you give me for my dinner,
   If I get up today?

6. A nice young man with rosy cheeks,
   A nice young man with rosy cheeks,
   A nice young man with rosy cheeks,
   If you'll get up today.

7. Yes, Mother, I will get up,
   I will, I will, I will get up,
   Yes, Mother, I will get up,
   I will get up today.

   The players form a ring and skip around Lazy Mary, who sits or lies in the center. Those in the circle sing stanza 1, and Lazy Mary answers with stanza 2. The circle repeats stanza 1, Mary sings stanza 3, the circle sings stanza 4, Mary sings stanza 5 — and so on to the end. Then Mary rises, points to someone, and chases him in and out the circle until she tags him. The one she catches becomes Lazy Mary for the next game.

A-Hunting We Will Go

Oh, have you seen my Pa?
Oh, have you seen my Pa?
He lights his pipe on a window light,
Oh, have you seen my Pa?

A-hunting we will go.
A-hunting we will go.
What care we if bears there be?
A-hunting we will go.

A-hunting we will go.
A-hunting we will go.
We'll catch a fox and put him in a box,
And then we'll let him go.

The players form two lines facing each other and sing the song. While each stanza is sung, the two top players — those who head the lines — seize hands and run down between the lines. At the end of the lines they turn around, clasp hands again, and run back. Then they separate and run outside the lines to the foot, where they stay. The next two players do the same thing, and the next two do the same thing, until all the players have run.

Now the two lines join together to form a ring. They dance round, singing a final stanza of the song.

Did You Ever See a Lassie?

Did you ever see a lassie (or laddie),
A lassie, a lassie,
Did you ever see a lassie,
Do this way or that?

Do this way or that way?
And this way or that way?
Did you ever see a lassie
Do this way or that?

The players join hands to form a ring, and skip or march around a lassie, or a laddie, in the center, singing the first stanza. The circle stops moving just before the words, "Do this way or that?" At this point the center player imitates some activity — for example, planting seeds, sewing clothes, chopping wood, rocking a baby.

During the second stanza the whole circle performs the same action. At the end, the center player chooses a new lassie or laddie, and joins the circle. The game often continues until everyone has been in the center.

46

Marching Round the Levee

1. We're marching round the levee,
   We're marching round the levee,
   We're marching round the levee,
   For we have won the day.
2. Go in and out the windows, (three times)
   For we have won the day.
3. Go forth and choose your partner, (three times)
   For we have won the day.
4. I measure my love to show you, (three times)
   For we have won the day.
5. And now I have to leave you, (three times)
   For we have won the day.

The players form a circle around one player, It, and skip round him, singing the song. During stanza 2, It "goes in and out the windows" of raised arms, trying to go through every "window" in the circle before the stanza ends. In stanza 3, It chooses a partner. In stanza 4, he "measures his love" (finger length or arm's length — as much love as he wishes to show). In stanza 5, It bids his partner good-by and joins the circle.

The partner is now It and the game begins all over again.

Skip to My Loo

1. Flies in the buttermilk, shoo, fly, shoo,
   Flies in the buttermilk, shoo, fly, shoo,
   Flies in the buttermilk, shoo, fly, shoo,
   Skip to my loo, my darling.

2. Cat's in the cream jar, what'll I do? (three times)
   Skip to my loo, my darling.

3. Chicken's in the haystack, shoo, shoo, shoo, (three times)
   Skip to my loo, my darling.

4. Little red wagon, painted blue, (three times)
   Skip to my loo, my darling.

5. Dad's old hat got tore in two, (three times)
   Skip to my loo, my darling.

6. Pretty as a redbird, prettier too, (three times)
   Skip to my loo, my darling.

7. She's gone away, what shall I do? (three times)
   Skip to my loo, my darling.

8. I'll get me another one, as pretty as you, (three times)
   Skip to my loo, my darling.

Players join hands to form a circle, then skip around two players in the center, singing the first stanza. This couple soon chooses a third person. The circle stops skipping but continues singing while these three skip about inside the circle. Then the original two players stop and lift their hands in an arch. The third person steps through the arch on the word "Skip."

The couple now joins the circle, which begins singing the second stanza. The person left in the ring calls in two more players, takes one as a partner, and repeats the action as above. The game continues in this way till the end of the song — or through several singings of it.

Today Is Monday

This is fun to sing just as a song, but it is also comical to sing in "parts," as a game. To do so, count off or otherwise divide up all the singers to represent the different days of the week. Then sing the song. Everybody sings the first line and the last two lines of each stanza, and the appropriate "day group" sings the lines reserved for the special days.

[sing repeat phrases like this]

Today is Monday, today is Monday.
Monday, bread and butter,
All you hungry people,
We wish the same to you.

Today is Tuesday, today is Tuesday.
Tuesday, string beans,
Monday, bread and butter,
All you hungry people,
We wish the same to you.

Today is Wednesday, today is Wednesday.
Wednesday, sou-oup,
Tuesday, string beans,
Monday, bread and butter,
All you hungry people,
We wish the same to you.

Today is Thursday, today is Thursday.
Thursday, roast beef . . . (Back through
all the days and the ending.)

Today is Friday, today is Friday.
Friday, fi-ish . . .

Today is Saturday, today is Saturday.
Saturday, pay day . . .

Today is Sunday, today is Sunday.
Sunday, chur-urch . . .

Shoo, Fly

Shoo, fly, don't bother me,
Shoo, fly, don't bother me,
Shoo, fly, don't bother me,
For I belong to somebody.

I do, I do, I do,
But I'm not going to tell you who.
I do, I do, I do,
But I'm not going to tell you who.

Couples join hands to form a ring, facing inward, and all move round, singing. At the words "I do," one couple lifts its hands to form an arch. The couple directly across the ring moves toward the arch and leads the whole circle through. Finally, the couple forming the arch turns in under its own arched hands.

Now the whole circle faces outward, and all move round in this way, singing the first stanza. At the word "I do," a second couple forms the arch. The couple opposite leads the whole circle back through under this arch, and the players face inward again.

The game continues until each couple has formed the arch.

John Brown's Baby

John Brown's baby had a cold upon its chest,
John Brown's baby had a cold upon its chest,
John Brown's baby had a cold upon its chest,
So they rubbed it with camphorated oil.

Sing the whole song through. Then sing it through a second time, omitting the word "baby." Instead of singing that word, imitate the motion of rocking a baby. The third time, omit the word "cold" also, and substitute for it a gentle cough. The fourth time, omit "chest" — and touch your chest. The fifth time, omit "rubbed" — and rub your chest. The sixth time, omit "camphorated" — and insert a little sniff. Then sing the whole song through loudly, with all the words.

Three Rounds

Row, row, row your boat,
Gently down the stream.
Merrily, merrily, merrily, merrily,
Life is but a dream.

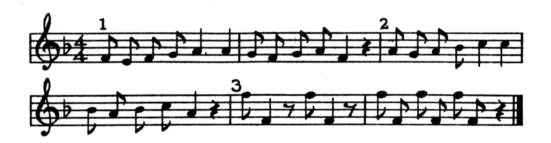

Sweetly sings the donkey,
At the break of day.
If you do not feed him,
This is what he'll say:
Hee-haw! Hee-haw!
Hee-haw, hee-haw, hee-haw!

Three blind mice, three blind mice,
See how they run, see how they run!
They all ran after the farmer's wife,
She cut off their tails with a carving knife,
Did you ever see such a thing in your life,
As three blind mice?

In singing these rounds, divide the singers into as many groups as there are lines in the round to be sung.

The first group starts the song and sings right through, again and again. At the exact moment when the first group arrives at *2*, the second group begins the song at *1*. This group also sings its way through the song, again and again. But it is always exactly one numbered step behind the first group. The third group starts at *1* when the second group is beginning at *2* and the first group is starting at *3* — and so on.

Sing as long as you have breath!

Old MacDonald Had a Farm

[sing repeat phrases like this]

1. Old MacDonald had a farm, E, I, E, I, O!
   And on this farm he had some chicks, E, I, E, I, O!
   With a chick, chick here, and a chick, chick there,
   Here a chick, there a chick, everywhere a chick, chick.
   Old MacDonald had a farm, E, I, E, I, O!

2. Old MacDonald had a farm, E, I, E, I, O!
   And on this farm he had some ducks, E, I, E, I, O!
   With a quack, quack here, and a quack, quack there,
   Here a quack, there a quack, everywhere a quack,
       quack.
   With a chick, chick here, and a chick, chick there,
   Here a chick, there a chick, everywhere a chick, chick.
   Old MacDonald had a farm, E, I, E, I, O!

3. Old MacDonald had a farm, E, I, E, I, O!
   And on this farm he had some turkeys, E, I, E, I, O!
   With a gobble, gobble here, and a gobble, gobble
        there,
   Here a gobble, there a gobble, everywhere a gobble,
        gobble.
   With a quack, quack here, and a quack, quack there,
   Here a quack, there a quack, everywhere a quack,
        quack.
   With a chick, chick here, and a chick, chick there,
   Here a chick, there a chick, everywhere a chick, chick.
   Old MacDonald had a farm, E, I, E, I, O!

For each additional stanza, add a new animal with the sound it makes,
according to the same pattern. Then repeat all that has gone before. Here
are some animals to add:

4. Pigs (With an oink, oink here,
        and an oink, oink there . . .).
5. Sheep (Baa-baa).
6. Cows (Moo-moo).
7. Horses (Whinny-whinny).
8. Mules (Hee-haw).

Miller Boy

Happy is the miller boy! He lives by the mill.
The mill turns round with a right good will.
A hand in the hopper and the other in the sack —
The girls step forward and the boys step back.

The players pair off, a boy and a girl together, and each takes his partner's hand. Now everyone forms a double ring, with the girls outside. The Miller Boy stands alone inside the ring, and all march round him, singing the song.

At the last line, the partners drop hands and do what the song says: Girls step forward and boys step back. After this is done, each boy tries to get the hand of a new partner, while the Miller Boy tries to break through the inner ring of boys and get a partner.

The boy who fails to get a partner becomes the Miller Boy for the next game.

RHYMES TO SAY

I had a little dog, his name was Ball;
When I'd give him a little, he wanted it all.

I had a little dog, his name was Trot;
He held up his tail, all tied in a knot.

I had a little dog, his name was Blue;
When I took him on the road, he almost flew.

I had a little dog, his name was Rover;
When he died, he died all over.

I had a little mule, his name was Jack;
He ran five miles and never looked back.

I had a little mule and his name was Jay;
I pulled his tail to hear him bray.

I had a little mule and he was very slick;
I pulled his tail to see him kick.

This little mule he kicked so high,
I thought that I would reach the sky.

I had a little mule, he was made of hay;
The first big wind that came blew him away.

Chick, chick, chatterman,
How much are your geese?
Chick, chick, chatterman,
Five cents apiece.
Chick, chick, chatterman,
That's too dear.
Chick, chick, chatterman,
Get out of here.

Way down South where bananas grow,
A grasshopper stepped on an elephant's toe.
The elephant said, with tears in his eyes,
"Pick on somebody your own size."

Why, the eye-dosity
Of your curiosity!
If I didn't have my kid gloves on,
I'd spank your bombosity.

Policeman, policeman, don't catch me!
Catch that boy behind a tree.
He took money, I took none;
Put him in the jailhouse, just for fun.

I stood on the bridge at midnight,
When the clock was striking in town;
I stood on the bridge at midnight —
There was no place at all to sit down.

I know something I won't tell;
Three little monkeys in a peanut shell.
One can read and one can write,
And one can smoke a corncob pipe.

Sam, Sam, the butcher man,
Washed his face in a frying pan,
Combed his hair with a wagon wheel,
And died with a toothache in his heel.

My father owns the butcher shop,
My mother cuts the meat,
And I'm the little hot dog
That runs around the street.

Oh, the funniest thing I've ever seen
Was a tomcat sewing on a sewing machine.
The sewing machine got to running too slow,
And took seven stitches in the tomcat's toe.

There's music in a hammer,
There's music in a nail,
There's music in a pussy cat
When you step upon her tail.

Fuzzy Wuzzy was a bear.
Fuzzy Wuzzy had no hair.
Fuzzy Wuzzy wasn't fuzzy,
Was he?

My mother bought a donkey — she thought it was a cow
She sent me out to milk it, but I didn't know how.
The night was dark and I couldn't see,
And that old donkey took a bite out of me.

Me, myself and I
Went to the kitchen and ate a pie.
Then my mother — she came in —
And chased us out with a rolling pin.

Did you ever hear such a noise and clamor?
The hatchet is fighting with the hammer!

I eat my peas with honey;
I've done it all my life.
It makes the peas taste funny,
But it keeps them on the knife.

I had a nickel and I walked around the block.
I walked right into a baker shop.
I took two doughnuts right out of the grease;
I handed the lady my five-cent piece.
She looked at the nickel and she looked at me,
And said, "This money's no good to me.
There's a hole in the nickel, and it goes right through."
Says I, "There's a hole in the doughnut, too."

Way down yonder, a long way off,
Where the bullfrog died with the whooping cough.
He whooped and he hollered,
He whooped and he coughed,
Till he whooped his head and his tail right off.

I asked my mother for fifty cents
To see an elephant jump a fence.
He jumped so high, he reached the sky,
And didn't get back till the Fourth of July.

I asked my mother for fifty more
To see the elephant scrub the floor.
He scrubbed so slow he stubbed his toe,
And that was the end of the elephant show.

Mary went down to Grandpa's farm;
The billy goat chased her round the barn,
Chased her up the sycamore tree,
And this is the song she sang to me:
"I like coffee, I like tea,
I like the boys and the boys like me."

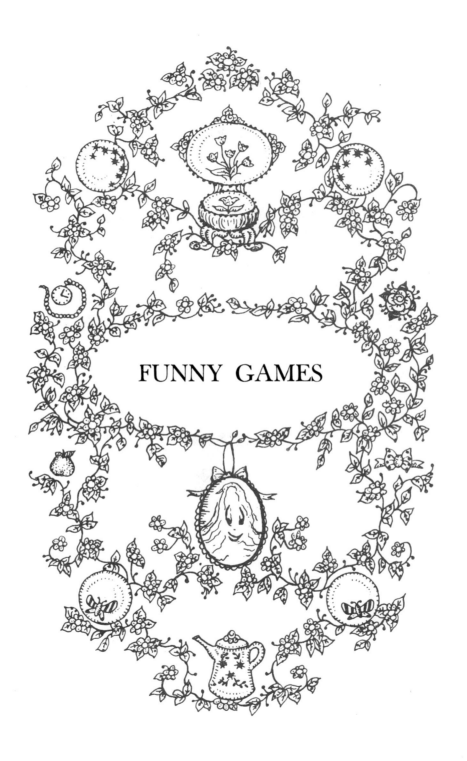

FUNNY GAMES

Ducks Fly

The players stand in a half-circle around the leader, who says "Ducks fly" and waves his arms. All the players quickly wave their arms. The leader then follows with "Snakes crawl," "Cats meow," "Horses neigh," "Wolves howl," "Lions roar," and so on. After each statement, the leader performs the action he names, and everybody imitates him. Anyone who cannot do so satisfactorily is out. So is anyone whom the leader can trick into a false action. He may say "Horses cackle" and cackle like a hen, but the players must wait quietly until he gives them a correct command.

This is a good game to play with forfeits. Then every player who makes three mistakes must pay a forfeit at the end of the game.

Simon Says

The players all stand or sit round the leader, or It, who makes a fist of each hand, sticks his thumbs up, and says, "Simon says, 'Thumbs up!'" The players must all do the same. Then It may say, "Simon says, 'Thumbs

down!' "— turning his fists over so that his thumbs point down. Or he may say, "Simon says, 'Wiggle waggle!' "— and wiggle his thumbs from side to side.

All the players must do exactly what the leader *says* to do, so long as he begins his command with the words "Simon says." But if he merely says, "Thumbs up!" they must do nothing.

The leader tries to trap them by omitting the words "Simon says" from his commands, or by himself doing something other than what he tells them to do. Any player who gets trapped in this way becomes It.

Going to Jerusalem

To play this gay and noisy game, arrange a row of chairs side by side so that one chair faces one way while the next faces the opposite way. There must be one chair less than the number of players who are going to take the trip to Jerusalem. A musician is also needed to play the piano or sing.

When the music starts, everybody marches around the row of chairs.

Suddenly the music stops! Then everybody dashes for a seat, and there will be one player who fails to find one. He is out, and he picks up a chair and carries it away.

The game is repeated for trip after trip until finally there are only two players and one chair left. The winner is the one who succeeds in getting this last chair.

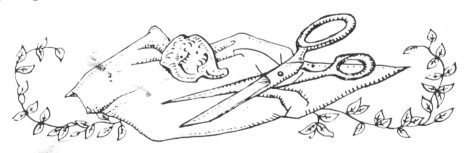

Rock, Scissors, Paper

This is a comical game that two or more players can play. It starts by someone shouting, "Let's play *Rock, Scissors, Paper!*" Then everybody faces inward and each player throws out either his fist, two fingers, or a flat hand. A fist represents rock, two fingers are scissors, and a flat palm is paper.

The rules are: Rock can break scissors, scissors can cut paper, and paper can cover rock. Each player looks at all the out-thrust hands to see whom he has won against and who has won against him. Every "victory" counts one point.

Each player keeps his own score through a series of throws. The one who first reaches a score of twenty-one wins the game.

Some players play a rougher game, however, in which all the winnings are taken out in "thumps." That is, after every throw each player gets to thump the wrist of the players over whom he has won. In turn he gets his own wrist thumped by any player who has won against him.

Ghosts

Nobody knows why it's called *Ghosts,* but everybody likes to play it. The first player thinks of a word and calls out its first letter. He does not tell the word. The second player adds another letter toward the same word, or toward another word. And so it goes round the circle until somebody is forced to finish a word.

The next player now starts a new word and the game goes on. But the unfortunate player who finished a word became a half-ghost, and nobody can speak to him without becoming a half-ghost, too. The half-ghosts talk to each other, and try to trap other players into talk.

If a half-ghost finishes a second word, he becomes a full ghost and is

69

out of the game. Anyone who speaks to him after this also becomes a full ghost.

Any player has the right, throughout the game, to challenge another player's letter. If the challenged player cannot complete a word by adding one or more extra letters to it, he becomes a half-ghost. But if he *can* do so, then the challenger becomes a half-ghost.

The game continues until everybody has become a full ghost except one player — who is the winner.

Buzz

In this game the players merely count rapidly in turn around a circle. But what makes the game so funny is that no one is allowed to say the number seven or any number that seven will divide into evenly.

If it falls someone's turn to say 7, 14, 21, or 28 (and so on), he must say "buzz" instead. Instead of 17, he must say "buzz-teen." Instead of 27, he must say "twenty-buzz." Whoever gives the real number when he should have said the buzz-number is out. If any players are left to say the 70's, they must say, "Buzz-ty, buzz-ty-one, buzz-ty-two," and so on. The winner is the player who stays longest in the game.

If you want to play a really hard game of this kind, then play *Fizz-Buzz*. In *Fizz-Buzz* you not only substitute "buzz" for every seven and its multiples; you also substitute "fizz" for every *five* and every number that five will go into evenly! Otherwise the rules are like those in *Buzz*.

Cat and Dog

Everybody sits in a circle. The leader holds up two small objects, say an orange and a fountain pen, which represent the cat and the dog. Then he passes the "cat" to his right, saying, "I found a cat."

Number Two takes the cat and says, "A what?"

Number One (the leader): "A cat."

Two hands the cat to Three, and says, "I found a cat."

Three: "A what?"

Two (to One): "A what?"

One: "A cat."

Two: "A cat."

Three hands the cat to Four, and the whole conversation takes place again — getting longer all the time.

But just after One started the cat going to his right, he started the "dog" going to his left, saying, "I found a dog." The same kind of talk went on about the dog as went on about the cat.

The game gets very complicated after the objects pass each other in the circle, because both sets of questions and answers must be repeated all the way back to One.

Poor Pussy

The object of this game is to prove that nobody can make you laugh — no matter how comically he imitates the antics of a cat.

Pussy is It. The rest of the players sit in a circle, and Pussy goes to each one in turn. Pussy crawls, purrs, meows, and otherwise imitates a cat in the funniest manner possible. The player before whom Pussy stops must stroke his head and say, "Poor pussy, poor pussy, poor pussy!" The player must not even crack a smile while saying this, or he must take the place of poor Pussy on the floor.

Forfeits

The old game of forfeits is very entertaining to play by itself or in combination with many other games. Either way, you need a Forfeit Holder and a Judge.

The Forfeit Holder collects a forfeit from every player. The forfeit can be anything: a ring, a hair ribbon, a pocket knife, a watch, a handkerchief.

Now the Judge sits down facing the players, and the Forfeit Holder stands behind him, so that the Judge cannot see the forfeits.

The Forfeit Holder dangles a forfeit over the Judge's head and says, "Heavy, heavy hangs over your head."

The Judge: "Fine or superfine?"

Forfeit Holder: "Fine" (if it belongs to a boy); or "Superfine" (if it belongs to a girl). "What shall the owner do to redeem it?"

The Judge names the penalty the owner must pay to redeem his forfeit. The penalties should be as funny as possible. Here are some famous ones:

1. Bark like a dog, meow like a cat, baa like a sheep, and bray like a donkey.

2. Laugh in one corner of the room, cry in another, dance in another, and sing in another.

3. Kiss your shadow on the wall.

4. Stand on one leg and count up to a hundred.

5. Say "toy boat" (or "mixed biscuits") ten times.

6. Put one hand where the other hand can't touch it. (Put it on your elbow.)

7. Eat a string rabbit-fashion. (That is, nibble it in without touching it with your hands.)

8. Smile (or frown) at everybody here in turn.

9. Pat your stomach with one hand while you rub your head with the other.

10. Say "What am I doing?" four times, accenting a different word each time. (The judge will say, "You're making a fool of yourself!")

11. Say the alphabet backwards .(You can begin at "z"; but if you're quick-witted, you'll turn your back to the Judge and start with "a.")

12. Put yourself through a keyhole. (Write "yourself" on a piece of paper first.)

13. Bite an inch off a poker. (Hold the poker an inch away from your face.)

14. Poke your head through a ring. (Stick your finger through a ring and poke your head.)

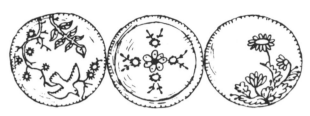

Spin the Platter

Your great-great-great-grandparents played this and it is still fun! One player is the Spinner and the rest sit down in a circle, on chairs or on the floor. Everybody takes a number: 1, 2, 3, 4, and so on.

Now the Spinner sets a round plate or pan twirling in the circle, calling out a number as he lets it go. The player with that number must catch the plate before it stops spinning, or he is out. If he catches it, then he becomes the Spinner, and the former Spinner takes his number and his place in the circle.

Uncle Joshua

It's hard to tell what is funniest about this game — the rhyme that goes with it, or the positions you get yourself into. The rhyme goes:

"My Uncle Joshua died last night."
"That's too bad! How did he die?"
"With one eye shut and his mouth awry,
　One foot held high, and waving good-by."

But you don't get to say it all at once until the end. Everybody sits in a circle, and the leader says the first line to his right-hand neighbor. The neighbor answers with the second line. The leader then says, "With one eye shut"— and closes one eye.

The neighbor repeats the rhyme up to this point with the next player, who repeats it with the next, and so on, until everybody in the circle has one eye shut.

The leader and his right-hand neighbor now repeat the rhyme from the beginning, as before. But the leader adds the phrase, "and his mouth awry"— and twists his mouth. The whole rigmarole goes round the circle as before. Now everybody has one eye shut and his mouth awry.

On the third round the phrase, "One foot held high" is added to the rhyme and to the action. On the fourth (last) round the final phrase is added: "and waving good-by."

Crossed or Uncrossed

People of all ages like to play this foolish game. You only need a pair of scissors — and chairs to sit on. No one except the leader knows the rules until after the game has started.

The leader starts by saying, "I am going to pass you the scissors crossed or uncrossed. You must watch what I do. Then you must pass them on, correctly crossed or uncrossed."

So the leader makes a great to-do of opening and shutting the scissors. Finally, he passes them on, open or shut. At the same time, he says *either,* "I pass them to you crossed," *or,* "I pass them to you uncrossed." It makes no difference which he says, because his *feet* are what he crosses or leaves uncrossed. But it will take some time for each player to figure this out.

Meanwhile, the player he hands the scissors to tries to solve the problem by crossing or uncrossing them and passing them on with the correct statement. Those who see through the trick will help the leader baffle the rest as long as possible.

The Giraffes and the Pig

If you want to give a piece of candy to everybody at a party, here's a funny way to do it. Announce that you will give candy to the person who can imitate an animal cry the loudest. Then whisper to one person the word "pig" and whisper the word "giraffe" to everybody else. Caution everyone not to tell his animal name.

Now say: "When I count to three, make the cry of your animal. But the person I've named giraffe must be silent, because giraffes can make no sound. The giraffe will get a piece of candy anyway. One, two, three!"

Everyone will be surprised to hear only one person cry out "Oink!"—or some such cry. And the "pig" will be more astonished than anyone else.

Coffee Pot

One player is sent out of the room long enough for the rest to select an action word like swim, dance, run, jump, sleep — or any other. Then he is called back to try to guess the word. He can ask anybody any question he wants to, so long as he uses the term "coffee pot" instead of the word he wants to know. And everyone must answer every question truthfully, though the answers also employ "coffee pot" instead of the missing word.

Suppose the word chosen is "sleep." The guesser may ask, "Do you coffee pot at school?" The answer would have to be "No, I coffee pot at home," or, "The teacher won't let me coffee pot at school." Other questions might be: "Do you coffee pot outdoors?" "Do you coffee pot at the table?" "Do you coffee pot in your room?"

Finally the player who is asking the questions will guess the word. The next player to leave the room is the one whose answer gave the word away.

OUTDOOR GAMES

Cat and Mouse

A Cat and a Mouse are chosen. The rest of the players form a circle with the Cat outside and the Mouse inside. The game starts off with the following conversation:

Cat: "I am the cat."

Mouse: "I am the mouse."

Cat: "I'll catch you."

Mouse: "You can't."

Now Cat begins to chase Mouse in and out of the circle. The players all try to help Mouse by letting him go through their line. But they try to keep Cat from breaking through.

When Mouse is finally caught, he joins the circle. Then Cat becomes Mouse for the next game, and a new player is chosen for Cat.

Pom, Pom, Pull Away

Draw two lines about fifty feet apart. All the players except It stand on one line. It runs along in front of them, and calls out:

Pom, pom, pull away!
If you don't run, I'll pull you away.

Then the players must run across to the other goal line, and It tries to tag them before they arrive there. All whom he tags become catchers, and they must help him catch other players on the next run-through.

The game goes on until everybody has been caught. The first one who was tagged is It for the next game.

Red Rover

This is the same game as *Pom, Pom, Pull Away,* except that the catcher is called Red Rover and the signal rhyme is different. Here, to start the players running, It calls out:

Red Rover, Red Rover,
Oh, won't you come over?

Players, when they are caught, help catch the others, and the first one caught becomes Red Rover in the next game.

Broom Walk

Boys form one line, girls another. The lines stand facing each other, while the player who is It walks around between the lines, imitating the actions of a sweeper. He chants:

1, 2, 3, 4, 5, 6, 7,
Where's my partner? Nine, ten, 'leven.
San Francisco, California! (Shouted.)
That is where you'll have to go.

As he shouts "San Francisco," everyone, including It, dashes for a partner. Whoever fails to get one is It for the next game. Before starting over again, however, the couples skip round in a ring, all chanting the rhyme.

If there are more boys than girls, you can have several Sweepers or Its. If there are more girls than boys, the Sweeper or Sweepers can be girls.

Poison

Draw a "poison ring" on the ground about four feet across. All the players join hands in a circle about this poison ring and start tugging at each other to force some unfortunate player to step into it. As soon as one does this, the rest break hands, shout "You're poison!" and run for safety. The poisoned one tries to poison others by tagging them. Whoever gets tagged joins the prisoner and helps to tag the rest of the players.

Players are safe only when they are touching wood. Even a chip of wood will do, but no one must pick up a chip or stick and try to carry it around with him. Nor must anyone stay long in one place. The game continues until everybody has been poisoned.

For a variation of the game, form the circle of players around a softball lying on the ground, instead of around a poison ring. The first player compelled to touch the softball is poisoned. The rest are poisoned by being touched with the ball.

Flying Dutchmen

This game is played like *Drop the Handkerchief*, except that two players always run — and there is no handkerchief! Everybody joins hands to form a large circle. The circle is made up of first a boy, then a girl, and so on. Two players, a girl and a boy, clasp hands and run swiftly round the circle. They are the Flying Dutchmen. Suddenly one of them strikes a pair of hands, and that couple dashes round the circle in the opposite direction. The couple reaching the empty spaces first joins the circle. The other two players are the Flying Dutchmen for the next game.

Charley Over the Water

The players join hands and circle around "Charley," chanting,

> Charley over the water,
> Charley over the sea,
> Charley caught a blackbird,
> But he can't catch *me!*

On the word "me" the players loosen hands and stoop far over. Charley tries to tag one on the back before he succeeds in stooping over. Anyone who gets tagged becomes It for the next game.

Wolf

This is a game to play on a stairway which has at least twelve steps. One player is chosen to be the Wolf. The Wolf sits on the top step and the rest sit at the bottom. The Wolf moves down one step every time he answers a question. Here are the questions and the Wolf's answers:

"Are you up yet, Mr. Wolf? It's one o'clock."
"I'm just getting up."

"Are you up yet, Mr. Wolf? It's two o'clock."
"I'm tying my tie."

"Are you up yet, Mr. Wolf? It's three o'clock."
"I'm combing my hair."

"Are you up yet, Mr. Wolf? It's four o'clock."
"I'm putting on my socks."

"Are you up yet, Mr. Wolf? It's five o'clock."
"I'm putting on my shoes."

"Are you up yet, Mr. Wolf? It's six o'clock."
"I'm brushing my teeth."

"Are you up yet, Mr. Wolf? It's seven o'clock."
"I'm drinking my coffee."

"Are you up yet, Mr. Wolf? It's eight o'clock."
"I'm eating my toast."

"Are you up yet, Mr. Wolf? It's nine o'clock."
"I've just finished my breakfast."

"Are you up yet, Mr. Wolf? It's ten o'clock."
"I'm putting on my coat."

"Are you up yet, Mr. Wolf? It's eleven o'clock."
"I'm taking down my sword."

"Are you up yet, Mr. Wolf? It's twelve o'clock."
"I'm coming after you!"

When the Wolf reaches the last line, he springs at the players. They must not get up until he springs. He chases them until he catches one — who must be Wolf in the next game.

Fox and Geese

A deep snowfall provides an especially good field for *Fox and Geese*. Tramp down the snow in paths to make a big wheel with spokes and a hub. Choose one player to be the Fox. The rest of the players are Geese.

The Fox tries to catch the Geese, and the first Goose he catches must become the Fox. Every player must keep inside the paths. A Goose who steps off a path is "caught," and if the Fox steps off a path he must catch two geese to get out of being the Fox.

The only safety for a Goose is in the hub. But this is a safety zone for not more than two Geese at a time.

Lemonade

This wonderful old game is also called *Trades,* because the players must imitate the work that people do in a series of trades or occupations.

First choose sides, which then line up facing each other along lines drawn fifty to one hundred feet apart. The players on one side select a trade and then march across the space toward the other line. As they march, the following conversation takes place:

Challengers:	"Here we come."
Other side:	"Where from?"
Challengers:	"New York."
Other side:	"What's your name?"
Challengers:	"Puddin' Tame."
Other side:	"What's your number?"
Challengers:	"Cucumber."
Other side:	"What's your trade?"
Challengers:	"Lemonade."
Other side:	"Show us some."

The challengers now pantomime or imitate their trade in all the ways they can think of. The other side watches what they do and tries to guess the trade they are imitating. As soon as the trade is guessed, the challengers dart for their home line, with the players from the other side in swift pursuit. A pursuer has only to touch a challenger to capture him. The captives join the side of their captors, whose turn it is to choose a trade and become the challengers.

When one side has captured all the players from the other side, the game is over.

Tag

Anybody can start a game of *Tag* by tapping (tagging) anyone else and saying, "You're It." Then everybody runs tauntingly about It, and It must tag someone to get out of being It. A player *may* cross his fingers and say, "King's X! You can't tag me." But this is not considered proper unless a player has stumbled and fallen or has met with some other trouble except the mere danger of being caught.

The game stops whenever the players get tired, or whenever It decides he can't catch anyone and says, "I give up."

Red Light

In this very popular game, one player is chosen to be the Red Light. The rest all line up at a starting line. Red Light stands some distance in front of the players with his back to them and counts rapidly to ten. When he reaches ten, he shouts "Red Light!" and turns around. While he is still counting, all the players run toward him, hoping to tap his back and start back to the goal line before he finishes.

But when he says "Red Light!" all must stop absolutely still. In a moment he says, "Run!" Now everybody runs for the goal with Red Light in pursuit. If he catches someone, the player must be Red Light in the next game.

Pig in a Hole

The "pig" is a ball or can. Each player has a stout stick, with which he digs out a small "stick hole." The stick holes are made in a circle around a larger center hole for the pig. There is a stick hole for every player except the one chosen to be It.

It tries to drive the pig into the "pig's hole" and everybody else tries to knock it away. But the fun comes from the fact that any player — including It — can thrust his stick into any empty stick hole. So a player who has been striking at the pig may turn around and find that someone else has occupied his stick hole. Any player who finds himself without a stick hole becomes It.

If It manages to drive the pig into the pig's hole, he wins the game.

Ring-a-Leavy-O

This is a favorite game of boys and girls who live in cities, but it can be played anywhere. All you need are some hiding places and a small circle or square to use for a "den."

Two leaders choose up sides — one side to hide and another side to hunt. The hunters must all stand in the den until the rest are hidden and their leader cries out, "Ready!" Now the hunters go out in search of captives, leaving one player at the den to serve as a guardian.

To bring in a captive, a hunter must find one of the hiders and hold onto him long enough to shout, "One, two, three, Ring-a-Leavy-O!" If the captive has not managed to get loose, the hunter can lead him quietly back to the den. The captive must stay there unless one of his own side rescues him.

To rescue a captive, a player on his side must rush out of hiding long enough to stick both feet into the den and tag the captive — without being caught himself.

The game continues until all the hiders are caught.

Barley Break

To play this ancient harvest game, divide a long strip of ground into three parts as shown. The players form couples, and one couple links arms and becomes guardians of the barley field. These two players may not step outside their field.

The other couples stand in the two adjoining fields. They need not link arms. Various couples then advance into the barley field, where they dance around trampling the barley and taunting the guardians by calling "Barley break!" The guardians, always with arms linked, must try to catch the invaders. When one member of a couple is caught, he must stand idly in the field until his partner is caught, too. But the partner may return to his home field, and later come back and invade the barley field alone. When finally both members of an invading couple are caught, they must link arms and help the guardians catch others.

The game ends when all the invaders are caught. The first couple caught become guardians of the barley field in the next game.

Hopscotch

Hopscotch has been a popular game in many countries for hundreds of years. Here is one of many ways to play it.

First, make a court and fill it with numbers, as shown. Then find a piece of wood or other material suitable for a "puck" to kick through the numbered spaces.

The first player tosses his puck into space 1, hops in after it, and kicks it into space 2. He then hops into space 2, kicks the puck to space 3, and so on, until he reaches space 10. Now he changes feet and kicks the puck back from space to space in the same way until he finally reaches space 1.

If the player succeeds in doing all this without a misstep, he will win the game. But if at any time his foot touches a line, or he kicks the puck too far or not far enough, or his *other* foot touches the ground, he must pick up his puck and leave the court. The next player now has a chance to try. When the first player's turn comes again, he tosses the puck into the space where he "went out" the first time, and if the toss is successful he continues from there.

Any number can play, and the winner is the one who first makes a complete round of the court.

Giant Steps

Choose a leader, who stands on one line, with the players lined up on another line twenty to forty feet in front of him. The leader then starts telling the players, in any order, how they may move forward to his line and return to their home line.

He tells each player how many steps (one to five) that player can make at each move, and what kinds of steps. There are three kinds: Baby Steps (about the length of the player's foot); Steps (of regular size); and Giant Steps (as long as the player can make). For example, It may say, "Ellen, you may take one Step, three Baby Steps, and two Giant Steps." Then Ellen must say "May I?" and It must answer "Yes, you may" before Ellen moves.

All the players watch to see that Ellen carries out these instructions accurately. If she makes a mistake, she must return to the base line and start over again.

The winner is the player who first reaches It's line and returns home. He is leader for the next game.

Marbles

Here is the most popular of all marble games. Draw a ring about ten feet in diameter and put thirteen marbles inside to form a cross. The marbles should be about three inches apart. Each player also has a marble that he uses as a "shooter."

The players generally throw their shooters at a line, to see in what order they play. The player whose marble comes nearest the line plays first, and so on.

The first player "knuckles down" just outside the ring and shoots. If he knocks a marble outside the ring, he picks it up and shoots again. If his shooter stays in the ring, he shoots from the position where it stopped. But if his shooter stopped rolling outside the ring, he may "take roundsters" and shoot from any point on the ring. A player who fails to knock a marble out picks up his shooter and waits for his next turn.

The winner is the player who first shoots seven marbles out of the ring.

Crazy Relay Race

Mark off a race course between two goal lines, not over fifty or sixty feet apart. A room's length will do if you are playing indoors. Now choose up sides. The players line up as they are chosen, and they perform in turn.

Each side must have players run all the following races. Each race is run the whole length of the course and back. As soon as players on one side have completed a race, the next players on that side start the next race. Whichever side first completes the series of races is the winner.

1. Run a three-legged race. At the starting signal, the two first players on each team must tie their legs together, to form a single "middle leg," run the length of the course and back, and untie their legs. Then the next race can start.

2. Two players from each side run a wheelbarrow race.

3. A player from each side must run the course backward.

4. A player from each side must hop the course on one foot. If either player touches the ground with his other foot, he must come back three steps before continuing.

5. A player from each side must crawl the course on all fours.

If you have more than seven players on a side, you can think up any number of additional crazy races. Some suggestions are: hop round the course on two feet; hop, skip, and jump; a plain run.

Hide and Seek

The players choose It, who covers his eyes at a central base and counts by 1's or 2's to a hundred while everybody else hides. Then It shouts:

> Bushel of wheat,
> Bushel of rye,
> All not hid
> Holler *I!*

If anyone shouts *"I,"* It counts by 5's to a hundred and then sings out:

> Bushel of wheat, bushel of clover;
> All not hid, can't hide over.
> Ready or not! Here I come!

Then he starts hunting the hidden players. When he sees one, both start running for the central base. If It gets there first, he pats the base three times, saying, "One, two, three, for *Charley.*" But if Charley gets there first, he says, "One, two, three, for me! I got in free!" Any player who gets in free is safe from being It in the next game. Players all watch for a chance to come in free when It is not looking.

The game ends when all the players have been caught or have gotten in free. The first one who was caught has to be It in the next game.

Jacks

This game used to be called *Jackstones,* because it was played with stones. Now you play it with six little metal "jacks" and a small rubber ball. Here is the most popular version of the game.

Toss your jacks onto the ground or sidewalk and then toss the ball into the air. Let the ball hit the ground once. While it is bouncing, pick up one jack with your right hand; then catch the ball before it hits the ground again. Put the jack into your left hand. Now gather up the remaining five jacks, one at a time, in exactly the same way.

Scatter the jacks again. This time pick them up two at a time, bouncing the ball as before. Then scatter the jacks and pick them up three at a time. Scatter them and pick up first *four* and then *two* — or first two and then four. Scatter them and pick up first *five* and then *one* — or one and five. Scatter them and pick up all six.

It is fun to play *Jacks* alone, the object being to go through all the moves without a miss. When two or more players compete, they take turns; the winner is the one who completes the moves first.

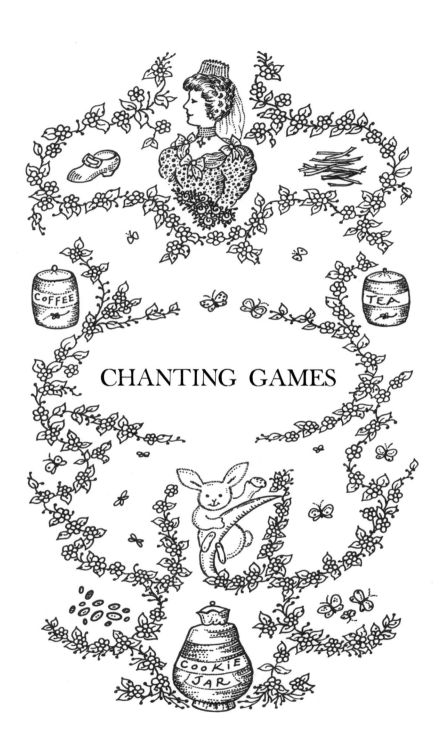

CHANTING GAMES

Bounce Ball Chants

One, two, three, O'Lary,
I spy Mistress Mary,
Sitting on a bumble-ary,
Eating a chocolate fairy;
One, two, three, O'Lary.

One, two, three, O'Lary,
Four, five, six, a buttercup,
Seven, eight, nine, a carnation,
T-E-N, I made it.

One, two, three, a nation,
I received my confirmation
On the Day of Declaration;
One, two, three, a nation.

Gypsy, gypsy, lived in a tent;
Gypsy, gypsy, wouldn't pay her rent.
She borrowed one, she borrowed two,
And passed the ball to Y-O-U.

Two, four, six, eight,
Meet me at the Golden Gate.
If I'm late, don't wait;
Two, four, six, eight.

A sailor went to sea, sea, sea,
To see what he could see, see, see,
And all that he could see, see, see
Was the bottom of the deep blue sea, sea, sea.

Once an apple met an apple;
Said the apple to the apple,
"Why the apple don't the apple
Get the apple out of here?"

Bouncy, bouncy, ball-y,
I broke the leg of my dolly.
My mother came out
And gave me a clout
That turned my petticoat
Inside out.

Skip, skip, to the barber shop,
To buy a penny candy;
One for me and one for you
And one for brother Andy.

One, eat a plum. Put your right foot over. One.
Two, touch your shoe. Put your right foot over. Two.
Three, bend your knees. Put your right foot over. Three.
Four, touch the floor. Put your right foot over. Four.
Five, reach for the sky. Put your right foot over. Five.
Six, pick up sticks. Put your right foot over. Six.
Seven, pray to heaven. Put your right foot over. Seven.
Eight, slam the gate. Put your right foot over. Eight.
Nine, get on the line. Put your right foot over. Nine.
Ten, this is the end. Put your right foot over. Ten.
    (Can be repeated for left foot; or right foot and left
    foot can be put over the ball in alternate turn.)

"Who took the cookie from the cookie jar?"
"Number One took the cookie from the cookie jar."
"Who? Me?"
"Yes, you."
"Couldn't be."
"Then who?"

"Number Two took the cookie from the cookie jar."
"Who? Me?"
"Yes, you."
"Couldn't be."
"Then who?"

"Number Three took the cookie from . . ." (etc.)

Variant: "Who put the cookie in the cookie jar?"
    "Number One put the cookie in the cookie jar."
    "Who? Me?" (etc.)

Bounce Ball or Jump Rope

"Hello, hello, hello, sir.
Meet me at the grocer."
"No, sir." "Why, sir?"
"Because I have a cold, sir."
"Where did you get your cold, sir?"
"At the North Pole, sir."
"What were you doing there, sir?"
"Catching polar bears, sir."
"How many did you catch, sir?"
"One, sir; two, sir; three, sir; four, sir; five,
   sir; six, sir; seven, sir; eight, sir; nine, sir;
   ten, sir."
"Good-by, good-by, good-by, sir!
See you next July, sir."

Alphabet Bounce Ball

A — my name is Alice,
My husband's name is Andy,
We live in Alabama,
And we sell apples.

B — my name is Brenda,
My husband's name is Bill,
We live in Boston,
And we sell buttons.

C — my name is Carol,
My husband's name is Charley,
We live in Colorado
And we sell cucumbers.

And so on through the alphabet. The player turns a foot over the ball on each word that begins with the proper letter.

By another way of bouncing ball to the alphabet, the player makes up or repeats sentences in which each word (or almost all the words) begins with the same letter. Examples:

Extra! Extra! Extra! Every Egyptian eats exactly
  eighty-eight enormous eggs every Easter evening at eight.

Little lonesome Linda lost her lovely little locket
  late last night.

Jump Rope

There are many jump rope games, which vary greatly from place to place. The players in your block or neighborhood are apt to have their own special ways of playing. In general, however, the idea is to skip over the rope while somebody, or a group, recites a rhyme or chant. Here are a few of the thousands of chants that players use:

One, two, buckle your shoe,
Three, four, shut the door,
Five, six, pick up sticks,
Seven, eight, lay them straight,
Nine, ten, begin again.

Keep the kettle boiling,
One, two, three.

Andy, Mandy,
Sugar candy,
Now's the time to *miss*.

Old Man Daisy,
Why are you so lazy?
Up the ladder, down the ladder,
One, two, three.

I like coffee, I like tea,
I like the boys (girls)
And the boys (girls) like me.

Apartment to rent,
Inquire within;
When *A* moves out,
Let *B* move in.

Butterfly, butterfly, turn around,
Butterfly, butterfly, touch the ground,
Butterfly, butterfly, show your shoe,
Butterfly, butterfly, that will do.

The clock stands still
While the hands go around;
One o'clock, two o'clock . . .

Down in the meadow where the green grass grows —
There stands *Mabel,* as pretty as a rose.
Along came her boy friend, and kissed her on the nose.
How many kisses did she receive?
One, two, three, etc.

Lady on your one foot, one foot, one foot,
Lady on your two feet, two feet, two feet,
Lady on your three feet, three feet, three feet, etc.

My mother is from England,
My father is from France;
My boy friend came from the U.S.A.,
With a hole in the seat of his pants.
He gave me all his peaches,
He gave me all his pears,
He gave me all his fifty cents,
And kissed me on the stairs.
I gave him back his peaches,
I gave him back his pears,
I gave him back his fifty cents,
And kicked him down the stairs.

Teddy bear, teddy bear, turn around, round, round;
Teddy bear, teddy bear, touch the ground, ground, ground;
Teddy bear, teddy bear, show your shoe, shoe, shoe;
Teddy bear, teddy bear, show what you can do, do, do.
Teddy bear, teddy bear, go upstairs, stairs, stairs;
Teddy bear, teddy bear, say your prayers, prayers, prayers;
Teddy bear, teddy bear, turn off the light, light, light;
Teddy bear, teddy bear, good-night, good-night, good-night.

Hello, boys, do you want to flirt?
Here comes *Betty* in a gingham skirt.
She can wiggle, she can waggle,
She can do the split;
But I'll bet you any money
She can't do *this*. (Jumper stops rope with foot.)

I'm a little Dutch girl
Dressed in blue,
And here are the things
That I can do:
Salute the captain,
Bow to the Queen,
Touch the bottom
Of the submarine.

George Washington
Never told a lie.
So he ran round the corner
And found a cherry pie.
How many cherries
Were in that pie?
HOT PEPPER, one, two, three, etc.

Raspberry, raspberry, raspberry jam,
What are the initials of my young man?
A, B, C . . .

Mother, mother, I am ill;
Send for the doctor to give me a pill.
Doctor, doctor, shall I die?
Yes, my dear, and so shall I.
How many carriages shall I have?
Ten, twenty, thirty . . .

I'm a pretty little Dutch girl,
As pretty as can be,
And all the boys around the block
Are crazy over me.
My boy friend's name is Michael,
He rides a motorcycle,
With a pimple on his nose
And ten flat toes,
And that's the way my story goes.

INDOOR GAMES

I Took a Trip

The players form a circle, and the first player says, "I took a trip to the city and I bought an *umbrella*." Instead of "umbrella" he can, of course, name anything else. Then the next player must repeat what the first player said, adding another object to it. For example, he says, "I went to the city and I bought an umbrella and a *bicycle*." The third player says, "I went to the city and I bought an umbrella and a bicycle and a *lollypop*." And so it goes all round the circle, each player repeating the whole sentence and adding something to it. If a player omits any item or gets the order wrong, he is out. The player who stays in the game longest is the winner.

Hot and Cold

One player goes out of the room and the rest decide on a task for him to do when he comes back in. This can be anything: standing on his head in a corner; playing the piano; turning out a certain light. Then the player is called back, and he must figure out for himself what the task is.

Whenever the player comes near the object of his task, the rest say, "You're getting warm," or "You're getting warmer." When he goes away from it, they say, "You're getting cold" — or "colder." When he touches it, they say, "You're red hot!" When he finally does what he is supposed to do, everybody cries, "You're on fire!"

Pick Up Sticks

The "sticks" are toothpicks or wooden matches, and the game is similar to *Jackstraws*. Two or more can play.

All sit round a table, and each player takes two sticks to use in picking up other ones. Someone drops a large number of the sticks into a high, loose pile in the center of the table. Now the game begins. Each player,

in turn, removes as many sticks as possible from the central pile, picking them up one by one with the two sticks he holds in his hands. In taking each stick from the pile, he must not cause any other stick in the pile to move. Otherwise he must not only put back the stick he is lifting, but also loses his turn.

The game ends when all the sticks in the pile have been picked up. The player with the most sticks wins.

Earth, Air, Fire, and Water

The one who is It stands in the middle of a circle where all the other players are seated. He tosses a handkerchief into somebody's lap, and calls out "Earth!" "Air!" "Fire!" or "Water!" Then he begins rapidly counting to ten. Before he reaches ten, the player with the handkerchief must name a living creature that walks only on the earth, flies in the air, or swims in the water — depending on which word was shouted. Since nothing can live in fire, the player must remain silent if It shouted "Fire!"

Whoever fails to answer correctly in time must replace It in the center.

Gossip

At least a dozen people are needed to play *Gossip*. All sit close together in a circle. The leader very carefully makes up a sentence, not less than ten words long, which he whispers into the ear of his right-hand neighbor. The neighbor tries to whisper the same sentence into the ear of the next player. And so on round the circle to the last player, who speaks out what he has heard. Then the leader repeats the sentence as he first uttered it. You will be surprised at how a statement is usually transformed in retelling!

Twenty Questions

One player is sent out of the room long enough for the rest to decide upon some well-known object anywhere in the world. Then the player comes back in and must try to find out, by asking no more than twenty questions, just what the object is. Each question except the last one must be answered by "Yes," "No," or "I don't know."

Suppose the object chosen was the Mississippi River. The questions might go something like this:

"Is it in the United States?"	"Yes."
"Is it alive?"	"No."
"Did people build it?"	"No."
"Is it under the ground?"	"I don't know."
"Is it a food?"	"No."
"Can people drink it?"	"Yes."
"Is it a lake?"	"No."
"Is it a river?"	"Yes."
"Is it a great big river?"	"Yes."
"Is it the Mississippi River?"	"Yes."

Many objects, of course, will be much harder to guess than this one.

The game can be varied by having one player think of the object; then all the rest in turn ask *him* the twenty questions.

An old game much like this is called *Who Is It?* In *Who Is It?* the twenty questions are asked in an effort to find out the name of a famous person in history who has been decided upon.

Blind Man's Buff

One player is blindfolded. The rest of the players join hands and circle round the Blind Man several times and then stop. As soon as they stop, the Blind Man points, and the player he points to must step into the ring. The Blind Man then has to catch him and try to tell whom he has caught by feeling the captive's face. If he succeeds, the captured player becomes the Blind Man for the next game. But if the Blind Man mistook the player he caught for somebody else, he must be Blind Man again.

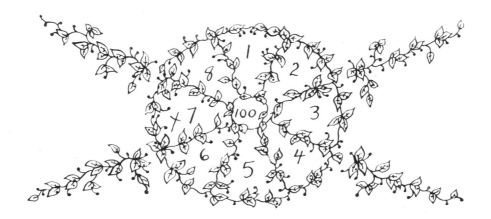

Tit, Tat, Toe

You need a pad of paper and a pencil to draw a circle. Mark the circle off with as many spokes as you like, and number the spaces between the spokes one, two, three, and so on. Make the "hub" circle at the center very small, and put the number 100 in it.

Now you are ready to play. Two or more can play. Each player in turn shuts his eyes and moves his pencil about above the circle, saying:

Tit, tat, toe,

Round I go;

If I don't miss,

I'll stop on *this*.

He tries, of course, to put his pencil down on the hub because the first player whose score reaches 100 wins the game. The space where any player's pencil falls is crossed out and cannot be counted again.

Zeroes and Crosses

This old-time game is also called *Tick Tack Toe,* and it is a kind of "between times" game, often played to fill in an idle moment between other games.

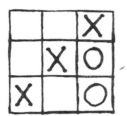

The picture shows how it is played. The first player puts an "x" in one square, the opponent marks an "o" in a second square, and so on. Each hopes that he will be able to fill in three squares in a row — up and down, across, or diagonally. If he does, he wins the game.

Dots and Lines

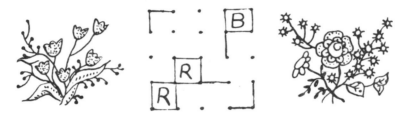

Make a square of dots, any size. Two people play, and each in turn draws a straight line, up and down, or across. The object is to fill in a complete box. Whenever a player completes a box, he marks it with his initial and gets another turn. The player who has the most boxes at the end of the game wins.

I Doubt It

In this game the players are supposed to bluff as much as possible. The object is to get rid of all your cards before anyone else does.

Deal out all the cards face down, one at a time. The player at the left of the dealer makes the first play. He lays one of his cards face down and calls out its number, for instance, "Three!" The next player now

calls out "Four!" and lays down a card. The next play is "Five," the next is "Six," and so on up to "King." Then comes, "One," "Two," and so on all over again.

But here's where the fun comes in. Any player who *doubts* that you laid down the card you called can say, "I doubt it." Then you must show the card you played. If you called it correctly, the "doubter" must take up all the cards on the table. But if you called it falsely, then you must take them all into your own hand. The player who gets rid of all his cards first wins the game.

Animals

Here is a game in which the winner gets all the cards in the deck. In fact, if there are over six players, it's better to shuffle two decks together for the game.

Deal out all the cards one at a time, face down. Before starting to play, each player announces the name of an animal. He must be addressed as that animal throughout the game. Then the game begins.

Everybody lifts a card at the same time, from his pile. Each person must turn his card *outward* and lay it face upward in front of his other cards. At the same time he looks around to see if anyone else has turned up a card with the same face value.

If two people both turn up, say, fours, each shouts out the other's animal name. The one who shouts first gets all the cards the other player has turned up so far in the game.

You can see that there may be trouble in remembering somebody's animal name quickly. A good idea is to select a name that is not too easy to say, like "rhinoceros." But no one should be allowed to call himself an Australian *ornithorhynchus!*

Old Maid

Take all the queens out of the deck except the Queen of Spades, and deal the rest of the cards out, one at a time. The object of the game is to get rid of all your cards, *in pairs,* and not to be left at the end of the game the Old Maid, holding the Queen of Spades.

The player sitting left of the dealer begins. If he has two cards that match — say two fours or two kings — he shows them, as many pairs as he has, and then discards them on the table. But if he has no two cards that match, he must draw, a card at a time, from the hand of the player on his left, until he can discard a pair. The next player follows the same rules, and so on all around the table.

The first player who is able to discard all his cards wins the game. But the game goes on until everybody is "out" except the one holding the Queen of Spades. That unfortunate player is the Old Maid.

Linked Letters

Here is a clever code for secret writing. You can quickly explain it to any friend, and then you can exchange written messages that no one else will be able to understand.

a b c d e f g h i j k l m
/ / / / / / / / / / / / /
z y x w v u t s r q p o n

Whatever words you want to write, spell them with the connecting or linked letters, rather than the real letters. For example, "girl" becomes "trio," and "boy" becomes "ylb."

Now decode:

1. Hlnv rmwrzmh dviv hrggrmt ilfmw gsv xznkuriv.
2. Orggov Qzxp Slimvi hzg rm z xlimvi.
3. Blf xzm'g ivzw dszg r dirgv.

Answers: 1. Some Indians were sitting round the campfire.
2. Little Jack Horner sat in a corner.
3. You can't read what I write.

111

Skip a Letter

Another famous way of writing in secret code is to substitute for each real letter the *next* letter that follows it in the alphabet. If anyone learns to decode your message, you can vary this scheme by substituting the *second* letter following the real letter, and so on. In fact, you can make up as many secret languages as you want to on this plan.

Now decode:

    1. J mjlf mpmmzqpqt.
    2. Mfu't hp txjnnjoh.
    3. Ecp aqw rnca dcnn vqfca?

Answers: 1. I like lollypops.
            2. Let's go swimming.
            3. Can you play ball today?
            (Here the second following letter was used, and "y" passed through "z," becoming "a.")

Number Code

You and a friend can agree on a code number with which to exchange messages. Suppose your number is 132. You write your message like this:

WHO IS SHE

132 13 213

XKQ JV UIH

For the "W," you counted one letter ahead in the alphabet; for the "H," three letters ahead; for the "O," two letters ahead; and so on. Now decode:

    1. UKCU LU NB JBW.
    2. TNCULPH LU GXP.
    3. SXP GDUU.

Answers: 1. That is my hat.
            2. Skating is fun.
            3. Run fast.

FUN WITH WORDS

Analogies

An analogy is a similarity. Read the first analogy below as, "Father is to son as mother is to_____?" Then fill in the correct word. At a party, it's fun to read these aloud rapidly and see who can write down the greatest number of correct answers.

1. Father:son::mother:_____.
2. Foot:shoe::hand:_____.
3. Hen:rooster::duck:_____.
4. Dog:pup::bear:_____.
5. Pencil:paper::chalk:_____.
6. Cow:calf::deer:_____.
7. Hat:head::coat:_____.
8. Sheep:lamb::frog:_____.
9. Hen:chick::fish:_____.
10. Balloon:gas::bicycle tire:_____.
11. Steamboat:engine::canoe:_____.
12. Scissors:cloth::razor:_____.
13. Bow:arrow::shotgun:_____.
14. Baseball:bat::tennis ball:_____.
15. Bird:nest::bee:_____.
16. Wheelbarrow:man::wagon:_____.
17. Ram:ewe::stag:_____.
18. Wolves:pack::fish:_____.
19. Gander:goose::fox:_____.
20. Horse:halter::dog:_____.

Answers: 1. Daughter. 2. Glove. 3. Drake. 4. Cub. 5. Blackboard. 6. Fawn. 7. Body. 8. Tadpole, or pollywog. 9. Minnow. 10. Air. 11. Paddle. 12. Beard. 13. Shell. 14. Racquet. 15. Hive. 16. Horse. 17. Doe. 18. School, or shoal. 19. Vixen. 20. Leash.

Word Pairs

Another good word game is called *Word Pairs* or *Affinities*. These are words used together so often that they seem to belong together. See how many you can find among the analogies in the last game. Here are some others:

Ham and eggs	Right and wrong
Needles and pins	Cash and carry
Cat and dog	High and low
Snow and ice	Collar and tie
Up and down	Thunder and lightning
Black and white	Adam and Eve
Comb and brush	Fine and dandy
Salt and pepper	Soap and water
Boys and girls	Hit and run
Hale and hearty	Fits and starts
Shoes and socks	Kith and kin
Come and go	Strawberries and cream

Make a list of at least fifty pairs. To play the game *Word Pairs,* a leader goes rapidly through the list, saying, "What goes with ham?" "What goes with needles?" etc. The winner is the one who writes down the largest number of acceptable answers.

Who Lost a Letter?

If you insert a certain letter the right number of times in each of the following lines, and separate the words, you will make a fairly sensible sentence. Each sentence will require a different letter.

1. NNEKNWSHWTGTTHEMN.
2. OODIRLSETOODRADESINRAMMAR.
3. OMEILLYBOYAYNONENEYLLABLEINCLA.
4. WIWIYWISONIKEITTEIYOFT?

Answers: Try "o" in the first sentence; "g" in the second; "s" in the third; and "l" in the fourth.

Crazy Sentences

They sound crazy now, but they won't be so crazy after you rearrange the letters of one word in each sentence.

1. Oh look at the evening tars!
2. Lemons grow on long vines.
3. Don't wear your old dagger clothes to the party.
4. The boys followed the dealer over the fence.
5. Better be silent than speak in range.
6. What a nice lather the white horse is wearing!
7. That mates engine can pull a whole train.
8. The deepest spool may be somewhat dangerous for you.
9. It is pleasant to eat fresh snub with butter.
10. Slide down the white poles on your sled.
11. The sheep are all horns in the spring.
12. This game can't salt always.

Answers: 1. Star. 2. Melons. 3. Ragged. 4. Leader. 5. Anger. 6. Halter. 7. Steam. 8. Pools. 9. Buns. 10. Slope. 11. Shorn. 12. Last.

Backwards and Forwards

See how many words you can think of that are spelled the same way backwards and forwards. One such word is "deed."

Answers: Here are a few: Anna, boob, dad, deed, civic, eke, ere, ewe, Hannah, level, madam, noon, peep, redder, refer, repaper, reviver, rotator, rotor, sees, wow.

Categories

This wonderful brain-teasing game is also called *Guggenheims.* It's very entertaining to play alone, but more fun to play with others — the more the merrier. The idea is to think of words which fall in certain categories.

	animals	cars	cities	sports	authors
H	hyena				
O	otter	Oldsmobile			
R				running	
S			Savannah		Shakespeare
E					

First make a diagram like that shown, and write a simple five-letter word — like *horse* — down the left side. Then list at the top five categories, or classes of things which belong together. You can list animals, vegetables, fruits, sports, automobiles, countries, cities, famous people.

Now you are ready to play. During the next five or ten minutes each player writes into the spaces of his diagram as many words as he can think of which belong to the proper category and which begin with the letter shown on the left. The diagram will show how this is done.

At the end of the agreed time everybody counts up his score. For any word a player has written that no one else has written, he gets 2 points. For a word that only one other person has also written, each gets 1. For words that more than one other person has written, players get 0. For each blank space, 1 must be subtracted from the score. The highest score wins.

Doubles and Triples

Fill in the blanks of each sentence with words which sound exactly alike, though they have different meanings and may have different spellings. For instance, if you had the sentence, "He looked into the_____sky and_____his whistle loudly," you could insert the words "blue" and "blew."

1. It is_____bad_____make_____mistakes in the same problem.
2. A boy with_____feet went into the woods to hunt a_____.
3. Mother_____me downtown with a_____to buy a flower with a nice_____.
4. You don't need a_____of knives to_____a single_____.
5. A fat man_____a large horse down the_____to the lake and then_____across it.
6. The woman takes her little_____out into the_____every day _____sunset.
7. It takes two quadrupeds to have_____ _____feet.
8. Did you_____your friend when you were carrying home the _____for dinner?
9. A farmer said, "I will_____my oats if you will_____a button on my shirt." His wife replied, "Is that_____?"
10. "They have a_____ _____at the zoo."
    "That's something that I never_____."

Answers: 1. Too, to, two. 2. Bare, bear. 3. Sent, cent, scent. 4. Pair, pare, pear. 5. Rode, road, rowed. 6. Heir, air, ere. 7. Four, fore. 8. Meet, meat, 9. Sow, sew, so. 10. New, gnu, knew.

Jumble Jungle

Here is a Jumble Jungle for you to find your way through. Each sentence that follows is a well-known saying or quotation. The first ten should be very easy to unscramble, because only the words are in the wrong place. In the rest, the words are all in the right place, but the letters are jumbled. Good luck!

1. Place a place and its for everything in everything.
2. The whole rotten barrel spoils one apple.
3. Don't try try first you again at succeed if.
4. A bridge don't come to it until you cross.
5. A soft snow shawl shoveled Sarah in softly.
6. Mice run three mice they three how blind blind see.
7. The laughs laugh and you with world.

8. Macaroni it feather he cap and a called in his stuck.

9. And a boy Jack no makes all play dull work.

10. Men came to the good party is now for all to the time of their aid.

11. A act yam kolo ta a gink.

12. A gib clabk gub tib a gib clabk reab.

13. A lofo dan shi yenom rea noso derapt.

14. Dribs fo a teefhar colfk heettrog.

15. Esh lless heessalls yb eth heessaro.

16. Eerhw saw ellitt osseM newh het stilgh newt uto?

17. YumptH typDum ats no a lawl.

18. Inne blimen blomneen blinbed bobny snut.

19. NodnoL Bigred si gallfin wond.

20. Ginkarb gosd erven ibet.

Answers

1. A place for everything and everything in its place.

2. One rotten apple spoils the whole barrel.

3. If at first you don't succeed, try, try again.

4. Don't cross a bridge until you come to it.

5. Sarah in a shawl shoveled soft snow softly.

6. Three blind mice, three blind mice, see how they run.

7. Laugh and the world laughs with you.

8. He stuck a feather in his cap and called it macaroni.

9. All work and no play makes Jack a dull boy.

10. Now is the time for all good men to come to the aid of their party.
11. A cat may look at a king.
12. A big black bug bit a big black bear.
13. A fool and his money are soon parted.
14. Birds of a feather flock together.
15. She sells seashells by the seashore.
16. Where was little Moses when the lights went out?
17. Humpty Dumpty sat on a wall.
18. Nine nimble noblemen nibbled nobby nuts.
19. London Bridge is falling down.
20. Barking dogs never bite.

Sign Writing

Make a key like this:

A	B	C
D	E	F
G	H	I

J	K	L
M	N	O
P	Q	R

S	T	U
V	W	X
Y	Z	

If you get a message written in this code, you can quickly construct the key and decode it. Now decode:

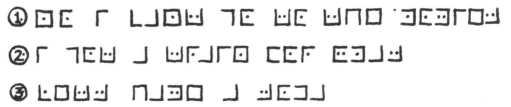

Answers: 1. No, I can't go to the movies.
2. I got a train for Xmas.
3. Let's have a soda.

Punctuate It!

Can you make sense out of these paragraphs by punctuating them correctly? They certainly don't sound very sensible now.

1. Said I I said you said said.

2. In writing paper and pencil leave space between paper and and and and and pencil.

3. That that is is that that is not is not that that is not is not that that is that that is is not that that is not is not that so it is.

4. Mr. Nott and Mr. Shott got into a fight Nott shot at Shott and Shott shot at Nott Nott was shot and Shott was not so it is better to be Shott and not shot than to be Nott and shot Shott not Nott shot the shot that shot Nott if the shot Shott shot had shot Shott and not Nott then Nott would not be shot.

5. *Somebody has already tried to punctuate this one — so perhaps you'd better start all over again!*

The new boy came into the schoolroom on his ears. He had red ear-muffs over his eyes, snow goggles in his mouth, bubble gum on his feet, stout shoes around his waist, a cowboy belt in each hand. He carried an apple for the teacher.

1. Said I, "I said you said, 'said.'"

2. In writing "paper and pencil," leave space between "paper" and "and" and "and" and "pencil."

3. That that is is. That that is not is not. That that is not is not that that is. That that is is not that that is not. Is not that so? It is.

4. Mr. Nott and Mr. Shott got into a fight. Nott shot at Shott and Shott shot at Nott. Nott was shot and Shott was not, so it is better to be Shott and not shot than to be Nott and shot. Shott, not Nott, shot the shot that shot Nott. If the shot Shott shot had shot Shott and not Nott, then Nott would not be shot.

5. The new boy came into the schoolroom. On his ears he had red earmuffs, over his eyes snow goggles, in his mouth bubble gum, on his feet stout shoes, around his waist a cowboy belt. In each hand he carried an apple for the teacher.

Word Magic

Transform one word into another! To do so you must change only one letter at a time, forming a new word that will take you partway to your goal. For example, you can change MAN into BOY in three moves:

MAN

MAY

BAY

BOY

Make the following word changes in the fewest possible moves. Then see if you can make up some new word changes of your own.

1. Change JOE to BOB.

2. Change MAN to NUT.

3. Change WARM to COLD.

4. Change DOG to CAT.

5. Change TWO to TEN.
6. Change LAMP to DARK.
7. Change GIVE to TAKE.
8. Change LOOP to POOL.

9. Change LOVE to HATE.
10. Change MILE to FOOT.
11. Change FIND to LOSE.
12. Change BOY to GAL.

Answers: 1. Joe, job, Bob. 2. Man, mat, met, net, nut. 3. Warm, worm, word, cord, cold. 4. Dog, dot, cot, cat. 5. Two, too, ton, ten. 6. Lamp, lame, lane, lank, lark, dark. 7. Give, gave, gate, rate, rake, take. 8. Loop, loot, toot, tool, pool. 9. Love, live, give, gave, gate, late, hate (or love, lave, late, hate). 10. Mile, file, fine, find, fond, food, foot. 11. Find, fine, line, love, lose. 12. Boy, bay, gay, gal.

EZ Does It!

Can U read these? Some R very EZ, and some R cra Z.

1. IV, LC, LN, KT, and RT 8 can D B4 dinner.

2. LC wants 2 B N avE8R.

3. Cats N K99 R NMEE.

4. R U N OT boy?

5. F U R MT, eat N ap L.

6. Pot ooooooo grow big N IOA.

7. *Conversation between two youngsters:* "*AB, C D BB?*" "*M R no BB!*" "*S A R 2!*"

8. *Who is this and where does he live?*

   Hill
   John
   Me.

9. $\dfrac{\text{Don't}}{\text{UU}}$ $\dfrac{\text{standing}}{\text{your}}$ $\dfrac{\text{and}}{\text{work}}$ 2 hard!

10. *The restaurant owner said:* I C U o o 4 U 8 o.

11. XQQ me 4 TTing U.

Answers: 1. Ivy, Elsie, Ellen, Katy, and Artie ate candy before dinner. 2. Elsie wants to be an aviator. 3. Cats and canines are enemies. 4. Are you a naughty boy? 5. If you are empty, eat an apple. 6. Potatoes grow big in Iowa. 7. "Abie, see de bees?" " 'Em are no bees!" " 'Es 'ey are too!" 8. John Underhill, Andover, Me. 9. Don't overuse your understanding and overwork too hard! 10. I see you owe nothing for you ate nothing. 11. Excuse me for teasing you.

Funny-grams

The leader reads out ten letters of the alphabet, which everybody copies down. Each player then writes a funny "telegram," ten words long, using the ten letters as initials. When all the players have finished, each reads aloud what he has written.

Suppose the ten letters given are N, R, O, B, P, D, E, R, H, F. One player might write: NINE RATS ON BOBBY'S PORCH. DOES EVERY RAT HAVE FLEAS?

Another telegram might read: NO, ROBERT, OUR BEAUTIFUL PIG DOESN'T EAT ROSES. HAVE FUN.

Where Do You Live?

The letters in these big American cities got jumbled. But maybe you can straighten them out. Each line represents a city.

1. No stob.
2. A talant.
3. Cry asuse.
4. Work yen.
5. Dire tot.
6. Lip dip heal ha.
7. Red ven.
8. Sal seen log.
9. Dance vell.
10. O belt I ram.
11. Hut soon.
12. Let teas.
13. Wont sing ha.
14. Aint us pal.
15. I sill love u.
16. Slew one ran.
17. I tall tacks ye.
18. A non slim pie.
19. Eu kwail me.
20. Yak it scans.

Answers: 1. Boston. 2. Atlanta. 3. Syracuse. 4. New York. 5. Detroit. 6. Philadelphia. 7. Denver. 8. Los Angeles. 9. Cleveland. 10. Baltimore. 11. Houston. 12. Seattle. 13. Washington. 14. Saint Paul. 15. Louisville. 16. New Orleans. 17. Salt Lake City. 18. Minneapolis. 19. Milwaukee. 20. Kansas City.

Hidden Words

In one of these squares you can find all your relatives, and perhaps some you do not have. In the other square you will find fourteen hidden animals. Here is how to look for them:

Start anywhere with a letter that may begin a word you are looking

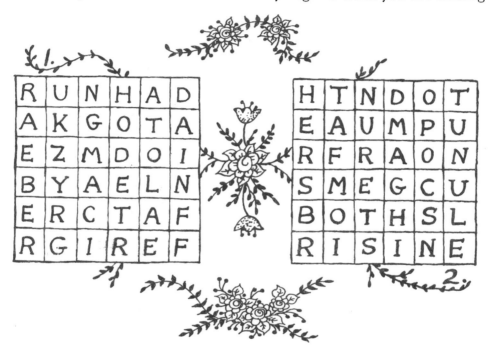

for. Move to any neighboring block for your next letter, and so on, until you complete a word. You may not use the same block twice to spell the same word; but you may use it again for spelling another word.

Answers: Square One contains monkey, camel, goat, bear, zebra, gnu, dog, cat, rat, hog, lion, tiger, toad, and giraffe.

Square Two contains grandpa, grandma, father, mother, brother, sister, uncle, aunt, cousin.

Thank You

You: "You count after me, and say the letter 'q' after each number."

Friend: "O.K."

You: "One."

Friend: "One-q."

You: "Two."

Friend: "Two-q."

You: "Three."

Friend: "Three-q."

You: "Four."

Friend: "Four-q."

You: "Five."

Friend: "Five-q."

You: "Six."

Friend: "Six-q."

You: "Seven."

Friend: "Seven-q."

You: "Eight."

Friend: "Eight-q."

You: "Nine."

Friend: "Nine-q."

You: "Ten."

Friend: "Ten-q."

You: "You're welcome!"

The Mysterious Word

A certain word has four letters. Take two letters away and you have four left. Take another letter away and you have five left. What is the word?

Answer: F I V E.

FUN
WITH NUMBERS

1089

702

594

The 1089 Trick

Have several people do this at the same time. Each should have a pencil and paper. Here are the directions, with two examples to show how the game works out:

	(1)	(2)
Write down a number with 3 figures:	702	389
Write this number backwards:	207	983
Subtract the smaller from the larger:	495	594
Write this number backwards:	594	495
Add, and you will always get:	1089	1089

The Stockings

A lady had twenty pairs of white stockings and twenty pairs of black stockings. She asked her small son to go up to her room and bring her a pair. He asked, "What color do you want?" She said, "Oh, either kind. Just be sure to bring two that match."

Her room was dark, but he found the drawer where she kept her stockings. How many did he have to bring back to be sure she would have a pair of the same color?

Answer: Three.

Magic Square

In the diagram you have nine spaces, and there are nine digits between 1 and 9. Put one of these digits in each space in such a way that the numbers in every straight row of three spaces will add up to fifteen. There are three vertical rows, three horizontal rows, and two diagonal rows.

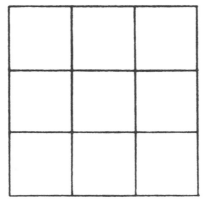

8	1	6
3	5	7
4	9	2

or

4	3	8
9	5	1
2	7	6

or

4	9	2
3	5	7
8	1	6

or

2	9	4
7	5	3
6	1	8

This Is Odd

Have someone hide a dime in one hand and a penny in the other. Now say, "I can tell you which hand you have the dime in." Ask him to multiply the value of the coin in his right hand by five, and the value of the coin in his left hand by six. Now ask him to add the two numbers he got and give you the total.

If the total is *odd,* the dime is in his left hand; if the total is *even,* the dime is in his right hand.

How Many Nines?

How many nines are there between one and a hundred?

Answer: Twenty. Don't forget to count all the nines in the nineties, including the two in ninety-nine.

The Hungry Bookworm

A friend gave you a three-volume set of the works of your favorite author for Christmas. You were too busy with winter sports just then to read the books, so you set them in order on your bookshelf — Volume I, Volume II and Volume III. But you measured their thickness carefully before doing so, and discovered that each book was exactly 1½ inches thick. One inch of this thickness was the text itself, and a half-inch was the thickness of the two covers. That is, each cover was one-quarter inch thick.

Now some months later you discovered that a bookworm had eaten his way through the books from page 1 of the first volume to the last page of the third volume. How far did he travel?

Answer: Two inches. He went through the front cover only of Volume I, the text and both covers of Volume II, and the back cover only of Volume III.

Frog in the Well

A frog is at the bottom of a well ten feet deep. He can jump three feet, but every time he jumps three feet he falls back two feet. How many jumps will he have to make to get out of the well?

Answer: He gets out on his eighth jump.

The Fast Trains

Every day at noon a train leaves New York for Miami and another train leaves Miami for New York. The trip each way takes twenty-five hours. If you left New York on one of these trains, how many north-bound trains would you meet on the way?

Answer: Three. Soon after leaving New York you would meet the train that left Miami the day before. About halfway you would meet the train that left Miami when you left New York. Just before reaching Miami you would meet the train that left there one hour before your arrival.

The Three Threes

Put three 3's together to make 4; to make 11; to make 3; to make 36; to make 30; to make 1/11.

Answer: $3\frac{3}{3}$; $33 \div 3$; $\frac{3}{3} \times 3$; $33 + 3$; $33 - 3$; $3 \div 33$.

When Is Your Birthday?

You can tell the birthday and age of any friend who can write down a few figures correctly on a piece of paper. The first thing he must do is write down *as a single figure* the date and the month of his birth. If he was born on the sixth of May, he writes down 65. (The 6 is for the day; the 5 is for the fifth month, May. If he were born on the fifteenth of December, he would write down 1512.) Then continue:

Your directions	His figures
Birthday and month:	65
Multiply by 2:	130
Add 5:	135
Multiply by 100:	13500
Divide by 2:	6750
(Suppose he is 12.)	
Now add your age:	12
	6762
Now add a day for each day in the year:	365
	7127

Ask him to read this last figure to you. You write it down and subtract 615 from it; and you will be able to tell your friend's birthday and age:

$$7127$$
$$615$$
$$6512$$

How Long Will It Take?

If five cats can catch five mice in five minutes, how long will it take ten cats to catch ten mice?

Answer: Five minutes. It takes each cat five minutes to catch its mouse.

139

The Fox, the Goose, and the Corn

A farmer started to market with a fox, a goose, and a bag of corn. On the way he came to a stream. There was a rowboat, but it was only big enough for the farmer to take one of these things across at a time.

He faced a great problem. If he left the fox and the goose on one side together, the fox would eat the goose. If he left the goose and corn together, the goose would eat the corn. How did he get them all safely across?

Answer: He rowed across with the goose and came back. Then he took the fox over and brought the goose back. Next he took the corn over. Finally he took the goose over again.

How Many Eggs?

If eggs cost 26 cents a dozen, how many can you buy for a cent and a quarter?

Answer: A dozen. (Don't a *cent* and a *quarter* make 26 cents?)

Houses

I counted twenty houses on my right one morning on the road to school. On the way back I counted twenty houses on my left. How many houses did I count in all?

Answer: Twenty. You counted the same houses twice.

Think of a Number!

Here is a little numbers trick that will baffle your friends. It is shown in dialogue.

> *Alice:* "Think of a number."
> *John:* "O.K."
> *Alice:* "Add seven."
> *John:* "O.K."
> *Alice:* "Double the number you now have."
> *John:* "O.K."
> *Alice:* "Subtract four."
> *John:* "O.K."
> *Alice:* "What's your number now?"
> *John:* "Thirty-eight."
> *Alice:* "The number you thought of was fourteen."
> *John:* "How did you know?"

Alice merely divided thirty-eight by two, and subtracted five.

The Clock

If it takes a clock two seconds to strike two o'clock, how long will it take it to strike four o'clock?

Answer: Six seconds.

Squirrel's Ears

A squirrel hides six ears of corn in a hollow log. Later he decides to take the corn away. How long will it take him to do so if he can carry only three ears a day out of the log?

Answer: Six days — because he must carry his *own* ears on each trip.

TRICKS AND SELLS

The Other Side of the Street

Next time you are standing on the sidewalk with a friend, offer to prove to him that he is really standing on the other side of the street. He will no doubt be glad to give you a chance to prove anything so absurd. So just point across the street and say, "That's *one* side of the street, isn't it?" He will have to admit that. Next say, "This is the other side of the street, isn't it?" He'll have to admit that, too. Then say, "So you are on the other side of the street." He won't admit that, but he will have to admit that you have trapped him very nicely.

A Game You Can't Lose

Here's a game you can't lose — at least not until your fellow player finds out the secret of why you always win. Play it with twenty-one matches (or cards or any other small objects).

Lay the matches down in a pile, and invite your opponent to play first. The rules are that each player, in turn, may draw one, two, or three matches from the pile. The one who draws the last match loses the game.

If he draws one match, you draw three. If he draws two, you draw two. If he draws three, you draw only one. In other words, whatever number of matches he draws, you draw enough to make a total of four. If you follow through in this way, your opponent will *have* to draw the last match, so long as he makes the first play in the game.

You can even risk making the first play yourself, so long as your opponent has not caught on to the principle of the game. Draw one match the first time, and then let him draw. But keep track of the *total number* of matches which both have drawn. Now, if, on your second draw or on any later draw, you can draw enough matches so that the total number of matches drawn is divisible by four, you can win the game.

Joke

Ask someone to spell the word "joke." Then ask him to spell "folk." Next ask him to spell "poke." Finally, ask him to spell the white of an egg. He will usually spell "y-o-l-k"— but the yolk is the yellow part of an egg. The white part is called albumin.

Cows in the Corn

A man missed his two cows and went to look for them. He found them in his cornfield — one was facing north and the other was facing south. How were they able to see each other without turning their heads around?

Answer: They were facing each other.

The Peculiar Peacock

You can ask a friend this question very innocently, as if you really wanted to know the answer: "If Mr. Jones owned a peacock and it laid an egg in Mr. Smith's yard, who would own the egg?"

After your friend puzzles for a minute, you can remind him that peacocks don't lay eggs.

Speak Fast

Have someone say these nonsense syllables very fast:

O wha

Tagoo

Si am.

The Beggar

A poor beggar's brother died. But the man who died had no brother. How could this be?

Answer: The beggar was a woman.

Kinfolks

Robert and Jerry went skating, and Jerry admired Robert's new skates.

"My Aunt Hattie gave them to me," said Robert.

"Who's she?" asked Jerry.

Robert replied, "Why, she's my Uncle John's sister."

"That's funny," said Jerry. "*My* uncle's sister isn't *my* aunt."

"She has to be, silly!" said Robert.

"You're wrong," said Jerry.

What kin was Jerry's uncle's sister to him?

Answer: His mother.

The Sick Chickens

You should be able to catch a friend on this joke. Say to him (rather rapidly), "A man had twenty sick chickens and one died. How many did he have left?"

Your friend will probably think you said *twenty-six* chickens and will answer, "Twenty-five." If so, you can soon set him right.

Raise Your Hand

If your friends don't know this trick, you can make them think you're a mind reader. Tell them that you can tell which person raises his hand when you are out of the room. Now go out and close the door. Call out, "Somebody raise one hand!" A little later say, "Raise it higher." Then say, "Now everybody, cross your legs." Then say, "Everybody, lay both hands on your knees." Now enter the room and glance quickly to see who has one hand much paler than the other. The hand that was in the air will be pale because the blood ran down. But *pretend* that you are examining the feet of everyone. Then finally point to the correct hand.

Monkey Business

To play this old trick you must find a friend who does not know it. Otherwise your intended victim will make a monkey out of you. Your friend must agree to say the words "Just like me" after every sentence you say.

You: "I went up one flight of stairs."

Friend: "Just like me."

You: "I went up two flights of stairs."

Friend: "Just like me."

You: "I went up three flights of stairs."

Friend: "Just like me."

You: "I went into a little room."

Friend: "Just like me."

You: "I looked into the looking glass."

Friend: "Just like me."

You: "And there I saw a monkey."

Friend: "Just like me."

A least, that's what you *hope* he says. But if your friend has played the game before, he will say, "Just like *you!*"

You Ate It

First Player:	"I one it."
Second Player:	"I two it."
First Player:	"I three it."
Second Player:	"I four it."
First Player:	"I five it."
Second Player:	"I six it."
First Player:	"I seven it."
Second Player:	"I eight it."
First Player:	"Oh, you *ate* a rotten egg!"

The Remarkable Letter

Robert Smith:	"I can write my whole name in just one letter."
His Friend:	"How?"
Robert Smith:	"Like this:"

The Coal

If a new furnace costs $200, what will a cellar full of coal come to?

Answer: Ashes.

Something Strange

You: "Want to see something strange?"

Friend: "Yes."

You: "Put your right hand over your left eye. Now put your left hand over your right eye."

Friend: (After a moment) "Now what?"

You: "Dark, isn't it?"

Is That Right?

You: "I'll bet you can't answer four questions in a row and answer them all wrong."

Friend: "I'll bet I can."

You: "Well, let's see. Are you an elephant?" (Or any other question.)

Friend: "Yes."

You: "Do you live in the zoo?"

Friend: "Yes."

You: "Do you eat hay?"

Friend: "Yes."

You: "Let me see. That's the fourth question, isn't it?"

Friend: "No, that's only three." (If he says this, he has answered a question correctly and you have won.)

Shell Game

Offer to show your friend (or a whole crowd) something no one has ever seen before and will never be able to see again. Your offer will probably be accepted. If so, take a peanut from your pocket, crack the shell, and ask, "Did anybody ever see this kernel?" Then eat it and ask, "Will anyone ever see it again?"

Donkey Business

A: "Let's play a game. You must agree to repeat everything I say,
except that when I say 'lock' you must say 'key' instead."

B: "All right."

A: "I am a gold lock."

B: "I am a gold key."

A: "I am a silver lock."

B: "I am a silver key."

A: "I am a brass lock."

B: "I am a brass key."

A: "I am a donk lock."

B: "I am a donk key."

Of course, B may call A a donkey instead of calling himself one.

Whose Pocket?

A: "I bet I have more money in my pocket than you have."

B: "I bet you haven't."

A: "Well, how much money have you *got* in my pocket?"

Don't Spill It!

Bring out two glasses partly filled with water and say, "I'll bet nobody here can balance these glasses on the backs of his hands without spilling the water!" Someone will be foolish enough to try. Have him hold out his hands palm downward, and set a glass carefully on the back of each hand. He will think he has won the challenge, but just let him hold the glasses there until he gets tired. He will be unable to get rid of them without spilling the water.

Pushing the Hat

Borrow somebody's hat and somebody else's finger ring and say, "I'll bet I can push this hat through the ring without even crushing it!" If anybody wants to see you do it, just lay the hat on a table, hold the ring near it, stick your finger through the ring, and push the hat!

Come Down!

Say to someone, "I can make my voice very powerful. If you will stand on this chair, I can make you come down by simply commanding you to." Someone is apt to think you can't do it and will climb onto a chair. Then say, "Come down!" When he comes down, you can remind him that he obeyed your command.

Blow Hard

Set a brick endwise on a table and offer to blow it over with your breath. But let everyone else try first. No matter how hard they try, they will fail. Now comes your turn. Just slip the closed end of a paper bag under the brick and blow into the bag. The brick will topple over easily.

This Ear

Here is a *double* catch — one you can work twice on the same friend, if he doesn't know it already. Walk up innocently to him, touch his ear, and ask, "Do you want this ear any longer?" Very likely he will say "Yes." You can say, "Then I'll *make* it longer."

After a minute ask the same question again. "Do you want this ear any longer?" He will think you are foolish for trying the same trick twice, but will probably say "No." Now is your chance to say, "Then I'll take it."

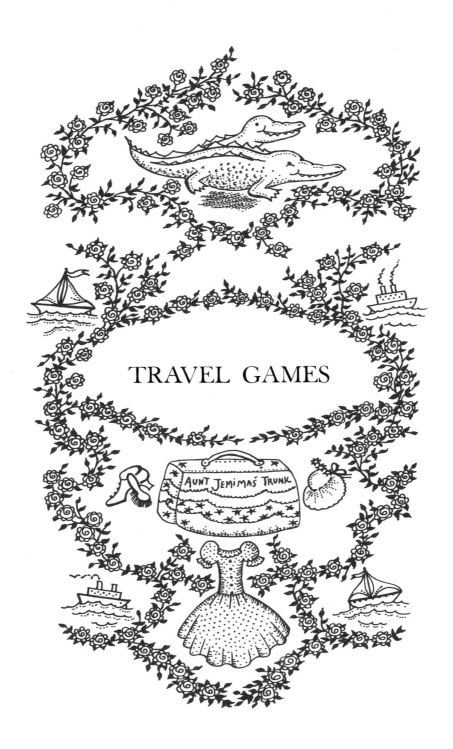

TRAVEL GAMES

Alphabet Travel

The first player thinks of a country, city or continent beginning with A and says, "I'm taking a trip to *Africa*. What shall I do there?"

The second player must answer with a verb and a noun that both begin with A — for example, *"Answer advertisements"* or *"Adopt alligators."* Then he continues, turning to the third player, or (if there are only two) back to the first: "I'm taking a trip to *Boston*. What shall I do there?"

The next player can say: *"Buy boats.* I'm taking a trip to *California*. What shall I do there?" And so on, as far as one can go through the alphabet.

Aunt Jemima's Trunk

This is a word game for two or more players, and it is about traveling. Imagine you are packing Aunt Jemima's trunk for a long trip. You can put anything you want to into her trunk. The first player says, for example, "I packed Aunt Jemima's trunk with a *calico dress*." The next player repeats this and adds something new: "I packed Aunt Jemima's trunk with a calico dress and a *shoe brush*." The third player (or the first one, if there are only two) may say: "I packed Aunt Jemima's trunk with a calico dress and a shoe brush and a *hat*."

Whoever fails to repeat the whole list and add a new item is out of the game. The winner is the one who can stay in the game the longest.

Hul Gul

Two or more players can play Hul Gul. Each starts with the same number of beans (or other small objects) to use for counters. Number One hides a few in his fist, turns to his neighbor, and says: "Hul gul!"

Number Two says: "Handful!"

Number One says: "How many?"

Number Two guesses. If he guesses right, he gets all the hidden beans.

If his guess is too low, he must give Number Two enough beans to make up the difference between the guess and the real number that Number Two had hidden in his fist.

Now it is Number Two's turn to conceal beans in his hand, and Number One's turn to guess. The game ends when one player has all the beans. Often a player will try to make his fist look big when he has put very few beans into it, so that his opponent will think he has filled it full. Children in ancient Greece played this game, and it has been popular ever since.

New Names

The players agree that for one hour or until the next stop they are all to have new names. These can be new real names, or to make the game funnier you can take the names of animals or vegetables or any other category of objects. After each player has selected a new name, whoever speaks to him must remember to use it. If anyone forgets and calls him by his ordinary name, or by any other wrong name, a point is scored against the one who makes such a mistake. The winner is the one who ends up with the lowest score.

New Words

You will need pencils and paper to play New Words. Write down a word that has something to do with a car, train or plane. Examples: "driver," "carburetor," "conductor," "whistle" or "propeller." See how many new words each player can make out of the letters in the word you choose. The word "driver" contains "red," "rid," "ride," "river" and some other words. You can't use a letter twice in a new word unless it appears twice in the original word. Proper names (like "Edward" or "China") or abbreviations (like "etc.") don't count.

The winner is the one who writes down the longest list of new words in a given time.

MIX-UP GAMES

See how fast you can play these games without getting mixed up! Each takes two players.

1. This is My Eyebrow

Put your finger on your ear and say, "This is my eyebrow! One, two, three, four, five, six, seven, eight, nine, ten." Before you reach ten, the other player must put his finger on his *eyebrow* and say, "This is my ear! One, two, three, (etc.)." Now, before *he* (or she) reaches ten, you must repeat what you did at first — and so on.

The loser is the one who gets mixed up first. The winner has the right to start a new game, naming other parts of the body. (For instance, touch your chin and say, "This is my elbow!")

2. Left, Right

Touch your nose with your left hand, and at the same time grab your left ear with your right hand.

Now touch your nose with your right hand and grab your right ear with your left hand.

See how fast you can do these things in turn. As soon as you make a mistake, it is another player's turn.

3. The Minister's Cat

There are two ways to play this funny game, and two or more players can play.

1. Each player must in turn describe the minister's cat with an adjective beginning with A. Number One: "The minister's cat is an *amiable* cat." Number Two: "The minister's cat is an *acrobatic* cat."

The player who can keep this up the longest then starts the whole thing over with B: "The minister's cat is a *brave* cat." And so on. Anyone who can't think of an adjective beginning with the appropriate letter is out of the game.

2. This is funnier, but harder, because you have to use the letters of the alphabet in turn and have to remember all the words that have already been said.

One: "The minister's cat is an *aggravating* cat."

Two: "The minister's cat is an *aggravating, big* cat."

Three: "The minister's cat is an *aggravating, big, cranky* cat." And so on.

You must fall out of the game if you fail to repeat every adjective and add a new one.

Acting Games

Here are some amusing acting games that you can play while traveling in a car, or anywhere. Two or more can play.

1. POT OF GOLD. You say, "If I found the pot of gold at the foot of a rainbow, I'd buy this." Then you show by acting out what you would buy. If you chose a puppy, you can whistle to it, pretend to stroke it, etc. If you chose a watch, pretend to wind it up. The others try to guess what you bought, and the first one to guess becomes the new actor unless the players have decided instead to take turns in a regular order. How would you act out a pony? A new dress? A bicycle?

2. HOW AM I ACTING? Think of a word that describes a way of behaving. The word will be an adjective: for example, "slow," "fast," "quiet," "loud" — many other words will do. Now the others begin to give you orders. If you chose "slow" and someone says, "Laugh!" you say, "Ha — ha — ha" very slowly. If someone says, "Turn your head," you turn it very slowly. The next player's turn comes when someone has guessed your word.

3. SIGN LANGUAGE. If the grownups complain that you are making too much noise, here is a way to keep right on talking without making a sound. You let certain signs stand for whole words: If you point to yourself, that means "I" or "me." Pointing to your eye means "see"; to your ear, "hear"; to your nose, "smell." If you want to say, "I hear an airplane," point to yourself, then point to your ear, and then make a zooming motion with your hand. How would you act out "I see a bird"? How many more signs for whole words can you make up to use every time you play this game?

Words, Words, Words!

Take turns making up sentences in which all the main words begin with the same letter. The funnier they are, the better! Begin with A and go through the alphabet as far as you can. Each sentence must have at least five words that begin with its letter, or you can agree on a larger number. You probably will have to omit X. Here are some samples:

> Agnes ate amazing apples at Aunt Annie's apple tree.
> Bill brought broken bottles into the back yard.
> Cousin Carol cooked cold cabbage.
> Zany Zed zeroed zealously into the Zanzibar zoo.

Hangman

Hangman is a game for two players, who need only a pencil and paper in order to play it. Number One thinks of a short sentence and writes down dashes for all the words. He will fill in the letters as Number Two guesses them. For the sentence I LIKE ICE-CREAM CONES, Number One writes down these dashes:

— —————— ————-———— —————

Number Two now starts trying to guess the right letters. When he guesses one that occurs in the sentence, Number One puts it on the right dash. When Two guesses a wrong number, One makes a mark against him, in the following order:

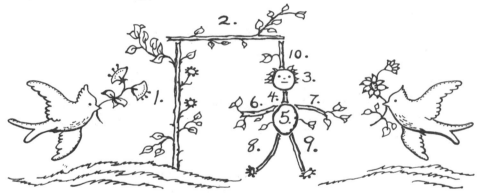

Number Two tries to guess all the letters before he gets hanged! If he succeeds, he becomes Number One for the next game.

Club Fist

The fun here is in saying the rigmarole and in seeing who can keep from laughing the longest. It requires at least three players, who must sit with their knees close together. One puts his fist on his knee, thumb up. Another catches this thumb in his fist, and so on until all the fists

161

are stacked up. The owner of the last fist raises it, and says to the owner of the next fist down:

"What have you got there?"
"Club fist."
"Take it off or I'll knock it off."

The fist is either taken off or "knocked off." The same conversation takes place about all the other fists down to the last one. Then the game takes this turn:

"What have you got there?"
"Bread and butter."

"Where's my share?"
"The cat got it."

"Where's the cat?"
"In the woods."

"Where's the woods?"
"The fire burned it."

"Where's the fire?"
"The water put it out."

"Where's the water?"
"The ox drank it."

"Where's the ox?"
"The butcher killed it."

"Where's the butcher?"
"The rope hung him."

"Where's the rope?"
"The knife cut it."

"Where's the knife?"
"The hammer broke it."

"Where's the hammer?"

"Behind the barn door crackin' hickory nuts, and the first one who laughs or shows his teeth will get a little box with five nails in it."

The "little box," of course, is a light rap with the hand, and the "five nails" are the fingernails.

Dumb Spellers

This funny spelling game is not as dumb as it sounds. The leader calls out words which the players, in turn, must spell. But each player must spell in a very unusual way. He calls out the consonants as in any spelling match, but he must not speak the vowels. Instead of saying "A," he raises his right hand. Instead of "E," he raises his left hand. For "I," he points to an eye. For "O," he opens his mouth and points to it. For "U," he points to another player.

Anyone who makes a mistake is out, and the winner is the one who stays longest in the game.

Spelling Backwards

This is another comic spelling game. When the leader calls out a word to spell, the player spells it backwards. All other rules are as for *Dumb Spellers*.

Chain Spelling

The first player selects a classification — cities, countries, first names of people, animals, foods, and so on — and spells a word belonging to that class. Each player in turn must spell a new word which begins with the final letter of the last word. For example:

SouP		RoberT
PeaS		TheodorE
SpinacH	*or*	ElleN
HominY		NaomI
YaM . . .		IvaN . . .

If a player misspells a word, or fails to think of a new word during the time it takes the last speller to count to ten, he is out. The game ends when there is only one player left.

RIDDLES

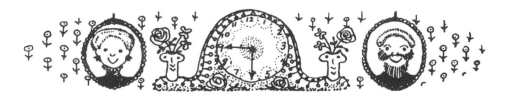

Why is a clock so shy?

> — *Because it always holds its hands in front of its face.*

How could you carry water in a sieve?

> — *Freeze it first.*

What has a foot on each end and one in the middle?

> — *A yardstick.*

Round as a biscuit,
Busy as a bee;
The prettiest little thing
You ever did see.   — *A watch.*

What is the difference between a pretty girl and a mouse?

> — *One charms the he's and the other harms the cheese.*

If you were locked in a room with no windows or doors, and all you had with you was a baseball and a bat, how would you get out?

> — *Strike one, strike two, strike three, you're out!*

What has teeth and can't eat?

> — *A comb (or a saw.)*

How can your pocket be empty and yet have something in it?

> — *When you have a hole in it.*

When is your neighbor's dog most likely to enter your house?

> — *When the door is open.*

Why are lazy people's beds always too short for them?

> — *Because they lie too long in them.*

What is the difference between a hill and a pill?

> — *A hill can go up, but a pill can only go down.*

What lives in winter, dies in summer, and grows with its root sticking upward?

— An icicle.

Railroad crossing! Look out for the cars!
Can you spell it without any "r's"? *— I-T.*

What goes round and round the house and leaves a white glove in the window?

— Snow.

When is a blackberry not a blackberry?

— When it is green.

Why do potatoes grow faster than other vegetables?
— Because they have eyes and can see their way better.

If two men go hunting and kill nothing but a jaybird, which they cook and eat, what is their telephone number?

— 281-J (Two ate one jay).

What goes all over the floor in the daytime and stands in the corner at night?

— A broom

In marble walls as white as milk,
Lined with a skin as soft as silk;
Within a fountain crystal clear
A golden apple doth appear.
No gates there are to this stronghold,
Yet thieves break in and steal the gold.

— An egg.

Why did the foolish man drive his car over the cliff?
— Because he wanted to try out his new air brakes.

When are your eyes not eyes?
— When the wind makes them water.

Why did they bury Washington on a hill?
— Because he died.

I have a little sister;
They call her Peep, Peep.
She wades in the water,
Deep, deep, deep.

She climbs up the mountain,
High, high, high.
My poor little sister,
She has but one eye.

— *A star.*

What land do very small children like best?

— *Lapland.*

Why does a milkman have white horses?

— *To pull his wagon.*

What is the best way to swallow a door?

— *Bolt it.*

How often does a caterpillar become very likable?

— *Whenever he turns over a new leaf.*

Why is summer like the letter "n"?

— *Because it makes ice nice.*

Why did the farmer name his rooster Robinson?

— *Because he Crusoe.*

Why did the foolish man take hay to bed with him?

— *To feed his nightmare.*

Why is a bad riddle like a poor pencil?

— *It has no point.*

When is a calf like ink?

— *When you put it into a pen.*

A word has five letters. Take two away and leave only one.
What is it?

— *St-one.*

Little Nancy Etticoat
Wore a white petticoat
And a red nose.
The longer she stands,
The shorter she grows.

— *A candle.*

What has four legs and flies?

— *Two birds.*

What flowers do you always wear?

— *Tulips (two lips).*

What has ears but can't hear?

— *A cornstalk.*

My face is marked,
My hands keep moving;
I've no time to play —
I must run all day.

— *A clock.*

How can you make a Maltese cross?

— *Pull its tail!*

What should you do if you found a horse in the bathtub?

— *You should pull the plug out.*

What is the difference between a jeweler and a jailer?

> — *One sells watches, and the other watches cells.*

> Red and blue and delicate green;
> The king can't catch it and neither can the queen;
> Pull it in a room and you can catch it soon.
> Answer this riddle by tomorrow at noon!

> — *A rainbow.*

Why is an elephant an unwelcome guest?

> — *Because he always brings his trunk along.*

Why does a cow go over a hill?

> — *Because she can't go under it.*

What are the biggest ants in the world?

> — *Gi-ants.*

Why do little pigs eat so much?

> — *To make hogs of themselves.*

What is lighter than a feather, yet you can't hold it ten minutes?

> — *Your breath.*

Where can you find a bank that has no money?

> — *At the river.*

Why should a man traveling across a desert always carry a watch?

> — *Because every watch has a spring in it.*

Why is a dog biting his tail like a good manager?

> — *Because he makes both ends meet.*

> Upon a hill there is a mill;
> Around the mill there is a walk;
> Under the walk there is a key.
> Tell me the name of this mill.

> — *Milwaukee.*

Why are the prairies flat?

> — *Because the sun sets on them every night.*

Why is the letter "d" like a squalling child?

> — *Because it makes ma mad.*

Why does a giraffe eat very little?

> — *Because he must make a little go a long way.*

How can you tell a thief from a church bell?

> — *One steals from the people;*
> *the other peals from the steeple.*

What gallops everywhere on its head?

> — *A horseshoe nail.*

Why did Tommy take a ruler to bed with him?

> — *To see how long he slept.*

What fruit can you buy from an electric plant?

> — *Currents.*

A boy saw a nickel lying on the sidewalk. Why did he run, instead of
picking it up?

> — *The buffalo scared him.*

> Uphill and downhill,
> It goes to the mill,
> Yet it stands still. — *A road.*

I met a man who had no eyes,
Who walked outdoors to see the skies;
He saw a tree with apples on;
He picked no apples off, he left no apples on.

> *— A man with one eye saw a tree with two apples on it; he picked one and left the other.*

Why does a hen lay so many eggs?

> *— If she dropped them, they'd all break.*

What runs but has no legs; has a mouth but cannot swallow?

> *— A river.*

What kind of an umbrella does the President's wife carry on a rainy day?
> *— A wet one.*

Why should we never gossip in a stable?
> *— Because horses carry tails (tales).*

If a pickle and a half costs a cent and a half, how much would one pickle cost?

> *— One cent.*

What kind of a table has no legs?

> *— A timetable.*

Look in my face and I'm everybody;
Scratch my back and I'm nobody.
Who am I?   *— A mirror.*

What has a big head but can't think?

— *A cabbage.*

What makes bakers the most unselfish people?

— *They sell what they knead (need) themselves.*

What has eighty-eight keys but can open no door?

— *A piano.*

What goes up every time the rain comes down?

— *Umbrellas.*

It's in the church,
But not in the steeple;
It's in the parson,
But not in the people.
What is it?

— *The letter "r."*

What does a cat have that no other animal has?

— *Kittens.*

Which side of an apple is the left side?

— The side that has not yet been eaten.

What seven letters of the alphabet did the little girl say when she was hungry and looked into the empty refrigerator?

— O-I-C-U-R-M-T.

There was once a little green house.
Inside the little green house
There was a little brown house;
And inside the little brown house
There was a little yellow house;
And inside the little yellow house
There was a little white house;
And inside the white house
There was a little sweet heart.

— A walnut.

If a room with four corners has a cat sitting in each corner, three cats facing each cat, and a cat sitting on each cat's tail, how many cats are there in all?

— Four cats: each cat sees the other three cats, and each cat is sitting on its own tail.

A riddle, a riddle!
A hole in the middle!   *— A doughnut.*

TONGUE TWISTERS

Box of Biscuits

MRS. SMITH'S
FISH SAUCE SHOP

How many tongue twisters do you know besides the following ones?

Two treetoads tied together tried to trot to town.

A big black bug bit a big black bear.

How high would a horsefly fly, if a horsefly would fly high?

Fred fetches fresh fish each Friday.

A cup of proper coffee in a copper coffee pot.

Six slippery snakes slide slowly South.

A mad manager imagined he was managing an imaginary menagerie.

Susie's shirt shop sells pre-shrunk shirts.

Of all the felt I ever felt, I never felt felt that felt like that felt felt.

See if you can say each of these short ones three times very fast:

> Red leather, yellow leather.
> Good blood, bad blood.
> Shy soldier.
> Seashore, seashore.
> Kick six sticks quick.

If two witches were watching two watches, which witch would watch which watch?

You can make up a tongue twister in rhyme from your own name or the name of any one of your friends:

> Annie, hannie, stick stack stannie,
> Dominecker, ten-toed, bowlegged Annie.
>
> Bob, hob, stick stack stob,
> Dominecker, ten-toed, bowlegged Bob.

Silly Sally Simpkins sold sixty shiny seashells at the seashore.

Red bug's blood and black bug's blood.

Men munch much mush;
Women munch much mush;
Many men and women
Must munch much mush.

The sinking ship sank.

Wicked witches will whisk switches.

"Mrs. Smith's Fish Sauce Shop," said the shiny sign.

Thirteen taxis took the tots to the train that took them back to Templeton, too tired to talk.

Francis found fifteen fancy filets of freshly fried flying fish.

Peter pared the peel from the pile of pears in the pail near the pool, then poked them with a pole.

A box of biscuits, a box of mixed biscuits and a biscuit mixer.

Feed fresh fish food to frisky fish.

Six thick thistle sticks.

Twixt six thick thumbs stick six thick sticks.

Chief sheep section.

Betty Botter bought some butter.
"But," she said, "this butter's bitter.
If I put it in my batter,
It will make my batter bitter.
But a bit of better butter
Will but make my batter better."
So Betty bought a bit of butter
Better than the bitter butter,
And made her batter better.

The sizzling sun shines on six swinging shop signs.

Peter Piper picked a peck of pickled pepper;
A peck of pickled pepper Peter Piper picked.
If Peter Piper picked a peck of pickled pepper,
Where is the peck of pickled pepper Peter Piper picked?

MYSTERY STUNTS

If you and a friend will learn these mystery stunts, you can mystify your friends at parties. It will take people a long time to figure each trick out.

Each is based on a simple system of signals which you two will know, but which nobody else is supposed to know. It's a good idea to change or vary the signals from time to time. You will think of many ways to do this.

You will also think of lots of ways to make each trick more puzzling and entertaining. You can add jokes, useless comments, an air of bewilderment — anything to throw your audience off the scent.

You and your partner should exchange roles frequently in performing these tricks. Let him be the clever one half the time!

White Magic

Offer to name any object selected by a group while you are out of the room. Your assistant, of course, stays with the party. When you return he will ask you, "Did we select *this?*" — naming one wrong object after another. To each question you answer "No." Finally he names the correct object, and you say "Yes."

How do you know when to say "Yes?" He names a *white* (or nearly white) object immediately before mentioning the correct one.

Then let him go out of the room, while the players select another object. When he returns, you query him. But this time, name a black object before naming the right one.

Shake Hands

Announce that you will leave the room and, when you return, be able to tell whom your assistant shakes hands with while you are gone. Wait awhile before leaving, until several people have spoken. Your assistant will shake hands, while you are out, with the one who spoke first. Name this person as soon as you come back into the room.

This and That

Go out of the room and let the players select an object, as in *White Magic.* When you return, your assistant will point to various objects and say, "Is it this one?" "Is it that one there?" "Is it this one over here?" "Is it that one?"

The cue will be the words, "Is it that one?" The first object your assistant points to after saying those exact words will be the correct object.

What Number?

Ask the players to select a number while you are out of the room. Suppose they select 61. When you come back, your assistant calls out a string of numbers, for example, 24, 32, 77, 61, 13, 80. The last digit of his first number tells you that the *fourth* number in his list is the correct one.

Where Were You Born?

Tell the group you have the strange power of being able to name the city where anyone was born. Then go out of the room. Your assistant will learn the birth cities of three people, before calling you back.

For the first person he will ask you something like this: "Was he born in Boston?" You answer "No." "In New York?" "No." "In Syracuse?" "No." "In San Francisco?" "Yes."

For the second: "Was he born in Oshkosh?" "No." "In Denver?" "No." "In Savannah?" "No." "In Cleveland?" "No." "In New York?" "Yes."

For the third: "Was he born in Santa Fe?" "No." "In Nashville?" "No." "In Kalamazoo?" "No." "In Chicago?" "Yes."

How did you know when to answer "Yes?" The first city he mentioned after a city with three syllables was correct for the first person. For the next person, he mentioned the correct place *second* after mentioning a three-syllable city. For the last person, he named the right city *third* after the three-syllable city.

This may sound hard, but it's as easy as one, two, three — and extremely mystifying!

Which Match?

Lay ten matches in a row on a table, and ask the group to select one while you are out. When you come back, your assistant will point silently, one by one, to all the matches.

You will know the correct one by this fact: He will point to it immediately after pointing to the match which lies farthest to his right.

The Mysterious Sentences

Everyone except your assistant writes a short sentence, folds the paper, and puts it in a bowl. The assistant pretends to do the same, but conceals his paper.

Now you draw a folded paper from the bowl, pretend to concentrate, and finally speak a sentence. Your assistant says, "That's mine." You unfold the paper, quickly read and memorize what is actually written on it, put it into your pocket, and say gravely to your assistant, "That's right!"

Draw another sentence from the bowl, concentrate again, and finally repeat the sentence from the previous piece of paper. Someone will have to claim this sentence also. Then unfold the paper and memorize what is on it. Continue in the same way several more times. You must stop while several sentences are left in the bowl, or someone may notice that there is one sentence less than the number of players.

The Talking Cup

Drop a coin loudly into a cup and say to the party, "This cup will tell me who takes the coin out of it when I leave the room."

Go out of the room until someone has removed the coin and the group calls you back. Now have everybody touch the cup in turn. Be sure to remember which *two* people touch the cup before your assistant touches it. And notice carefully which hand he touches it with.

Now pick up the cup and ask it, "Who took the coin?" Put the cup to your ear, listen carefully, and then name the person.

If your assistant touched the cup with his right hand, he touched it immediately after the person who took the coin. If he touched it with his left hand, he touched it *second* after the one who took the coin.

Invisible

Say to a group, "I have an invisible substance on my finger. But my friend here has eyes so keen that he can tell when I touch anybody's forehead with it."

Send your friend (assistant) out of the room. Then carefully select someone and touch that person's forehead lightly with your finger. Suppose you select a girl named Carolyn Smith.

Now call your assistant back, and let him spend some time looking at people's foreheads. Finally, say to him something like this: "Come now, show us how bright you are — or how silly!" He will "search" awhile longer and then name Carolyn Smith.

How did he know? You picked someone whose two initials were different from anyone else's in the room. Then you made up a sentence in which the first letter of the first word was one initial, and the first letter of the last word was the other.

Magical Ashes

For this one you need no assistant, but you do need to keep an honest face. Ask for a pencil and some slips of paper, and sit at some distance from the group. Ask them to call out, one by one, the name of a famous person. You write a name on each slip, fold it, and drop it into a bowl.

At the end, ask someone to draw a slip from the bowl. Burn the rest. Now ask the person who drew the slip to hold it against your head, while you try to "get" the name. At last say the name. Let someone unfold the paper, and you will almost certainly be right.

The reason: You wrote the second name that was called on every slip after the first one.

If you want to be *sure* to be right, then write down on every slip the *first* name that is called.

Nope

Go out of the room and let the players select any name famous in history.

When you return your assistant will say, "Is it Julius Caesar?" — or any name except the correct one. Answer "Nope." He will continue giving you false names as long as you answer "Nope." When you get tired of mystifying your audience, say "No" instead of "Nope." This will be the signal for your assistant to give you the right name, and your next answer will be "Yes."

Index by Titles